FANTASTIC FASHION

FANTASTIC FASHION

an illustrated history of the
bizarre and beautiful

Text by Barbara Cox, Carolyn Sally Jones,
David and Caroline Stafford

Concept by Ariana Klepac

APPLE

contents

introduction

Neanderthals painted themselves red. This possibly qualifies them as history's very first followers of fashion. It is easy to imagine that, thus rouged from head to toe, they would have dragged their knuckles with a little more swagger, basking in the envious grunts of rival fashion fiends.

So it has ever been. Cut, colour, elegance and refinement have brought delight to the discerning eye of the Assyrian temple maid, the courtier at Versailles and the rayon-draped American beauty. But better still have been the times – the many, many glorious times – when all pretence of refinement has been abandoned, along with restraint and sense, and with open arms and a broad, foolish grin we have embraced the extreme, the absurd and the often cruel dictates of Fantastic Fashion.

Periwigs, plate-sized ruffs, codpieces, loin cloths, platform shoes, panniers, leg-of-mutton sleeves, whalebone corsets, fake eyebrows made from mousehair – this book catalogues some of fashion's greatest triumphs and sorriest mistakes.

Beauty has always been in the eye of the beholder. That which is considered beautiful to one age may be almost sickeningly hideous to another. An ancient Egyptian saw a single eyebrow hair – sole survivor of painstaking all-over tweezing and shaving – as an abomination. The Victorian gent, on the other hand, cultivated his whiskers luscious and long, teasing and waxing them into elaborate sculptures. Medieval ladies padded their bellies to achieve that oh-so-desirable pregnant look; while the 1920s flapper starved that midriff flat to match the equally flat bust and derriere required for the straight-up-and-down tubular look, then considered gorgeous.

The pious and mighty have always been sniffy about fashion, regarding it as trivial, a sad parade of vanity, beneath their interest or even their contempt. If only they'd take the trouble to look again they'd realise that trouser width, skirt length, cleavage depth and heel height are the most accurate barometers we have of how people think and feel about, and their attitudes towards, status, wealth, philosophy, morality, religion, politics, art, science, nutrition, anatomy and sex – particularly sex.

And this is what makes the fantastic fashions of the past so compelling. What does the huge hoop skirt tell us about the life and times of the people who wore it? What does it feel like to be sewn into your underwear at the beginning of winter, never to be released until spring had sprung? When the gadabouts of the fourteenth century looked down at the toes of their shoes – 20 cm (8 in) long, pointed and curled – did they ever for a moment consider that such shoes are inherently stupid? Who does that guy in the flounced and powdered periwig think he is? Who is that woman in the space helmet and spike heels trying to be?

But more important than the hidden meanings and historical conundrums is the fact that fashion – and particularly fantastic fashion – is fun, and often addictive.

In every period of history, in every country there have been men and women who are not afraid to show the world in their choice of fabric, cut or pattern that they are reassuringly crazy. Long may they flourish, for they are the cat's pyjamas.

Right: In Erté's costume design for a woman dressed in black fur, we see an exaggerated version of the early twentieth-century, straight-up-and-down style, which became popular after World War I.

1
Shape Shifting

Fashion is
architecture:
it is a matter of
proportions.

COCO CHANEL, 1883–1971

Farthingales

Farthingales, notorious for being the most unwieldy and cumbersome fashion in history, first made their appearance in fifteenth-century Spain, when the ladies of the court began to sweep all before them by using hoops of rope, reeds or willow to stiffen their voluminous skirts. Soon this 'simple' stiffening of the gown was abandoned in favour of hoops of wire, wood or whalebone, used to lift and spread the skirts and ensure the wearer acquired the formal rigidity that was the fashion of the day.

Spanish Farthingale

It was in Tudor England, however, that the farthingale was to undergo its most extravagant transformation. Queen Elizabeth I had sent Philip II of Spain packing when he proposed marriage, but she remained deeply enamoured of the Spanish farthingale, adapting it over the years to her own purposes. By the end of her reign this extraordinary fashion had become a potent symbol of royal power and opulence.

Wheel Farthingale

It was the wheel farthingale of the 1580s that gave Queen Elizabeth the opportunity to stretch her glittering gowns to their furthest extreme.

Exclusively a style worn by the ladies of the court, the wheel farthingale was a huge frame, literally the size of a cartwheel, made of materials ranging from horsehair and rope to wire and whalebone. Over the hoop went layers of petticoats and, finally, the heavily embroidered skirt, which was gored to slope stiffly outwards, then drop vertically down to the floor to produce a tub-like shape.

The skirt parted to reveal the petticoat underneath, while a cushion at the back gave it a forward tilt which made the torso seem longer and the legs shorter. Any attempts at intimacy by an admirer must have been severely impeded by the fact that the object of his affection was standing in the centre of a wheel!

Above left: A demure Isabel Clara Eugenia of Spain models the relatively conservative A-line of the Spanish farthingale, sixteenth century.

Opposite: The extraordinary opulence of this court costume, with a heavily embroidered wheel farthingale, is worthy of Elizabeth I at the height of her power, but the portrait is thought to be of Catherine Howard, Countess of Nottingham, sixteenth century.

Prisoners of Fashion

Queen Elizabeth knew how important dress was in terms of manipulating her public image, and portraits show her in ever larger, more richly embroidered and certainly uncomfortable gowns. The queen's ladies-in-waiting followed the fashion with devotion but had to remember never to outshine their mistress. It was a lesson learnt the hard way by one unfortunate attendant when her farthingale, exquisitely covered in velvet and laden with pearls and gold, attracted a royal reprimand so sharp it seemed she ran the risk of finding herself locked in the Tower of London with an axe hanging over her head!

Elizabeth remained loyal to the wheel farthingale to the end, dragging the outsize dress from room to room as her ageing body became ever more emaciated, lying on pillows to prop up

Elizabethan Men's Bubble Skirt

Elizabethan men were patently unable to compete with the extravagant dimensions of the farthingale but managed a modest version of their own in the shape of the bubble skirt. They adopted the style of the doublet, which was heavily padded at the bottom and stuck out in a bubble or inverted heart shape. A well-turned calf, accentuated with garters, was a necessity if the wearer was to carry off the style with some aplomb. The bubble skirt reappeared in the twenty-first century, but this time it was worn by women.

Roll Farthingale

For those who could not aspire to the dizzy dimensions of the wheel farthingale, the 'roll farthingale' became a popular alternative. The 'bum roll', as it was known, was a padded roll in the shape of a sausage which was wrapped around the hips and tied at the waist with tapes. Rather more user-friendly than the full wheel farthingale, it too produced a tub-shaped hang to the skirt and achieved that all important, and almost certainly titillating, forward tilt.

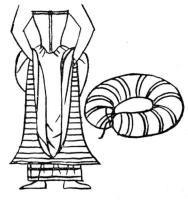

Left: The peplum-style bodice heightens the effect of the skirt, which has been bolstered by the bum roll (above).

its weight as if it might still bestow on her last days some lingering remnants of lost beauty and power. After the queen's death, the farthingale fell out of fashion and, although bodices remained firmly clamped, more natural flowing skirts replaced it.

Fashionistas in the Elizabethan Age had found in the expanding hoops of this extraordinary structure a way of establishing status and demonstrating wealth. It is clear from contemporary portraits, however, that most women look imprisoned by their huge boned underskirts. All too often the wearer of the farthingale resembled nothing so much as an ungainly hobby horse, tilting perilously towards earth with every faltering step.

Left: The daughters of Thomas Egerton, Ist Viscount Brackley, an English statesman, are dressed in identical roll farthingales for this portrait in about 1602. Any individual fashion sense is confined to scarves and jewellery.

Opposite: James I of England's doublet provided his torso with warmth and shape, and his hosiery with ties.

Panniers

Two hundred years after the farthingale made a hasty exit from the fashion scene, hoops once more made an appearance, but this time the important feature was width. Panniers, derived from 'panier', the French word for basket, originated in Spain but found their most flamboyant expression at the French Court of Versailles during the last years of Louis XVI's reign.

Packing Baskets

Panniers began as petticoats of heavily stiffened fabric, tiered with two rows of whalebone or osier rods and tied back with tapes. While the front of the dress was flat and the waist held in the steely grip of a stomacher, the split hoop was used to widen the hips and extend the skirt sideways in an elongated oval shape. The enormous influence of Versailles, where Marie Antoinette was able to indulge her whims and fancies, meant that whatever was *à la mode* in France soon became the fashion all over Europe.

The dressmakers of Paris were soon busily employed catering to extravagant royal tastes as the panniers were ever more richly decorated and embroidered and festooned with jewels. One rather exquisite gown looked ethereal but it was weighed down with 4 kg (8¾ lb) of silver.

In view of the extravagance of the fashion, it is hardly surprising that the wearing of panniers was a privilege restricted to royalty and a little coterie of high-born ladies. For these chosen few, the fashion was compulsory on state occasions, and failure to appear in full regalia in the presence of a visiting dignitary had the potential to spark a diplomatic incident. Only advanced pregnancy could be used as an excuse.

By the 1750s the panniers measured as much as 3 m (9¾ ft) from side to side and created a host of practical problems. Ladies of the court found it impossible to sit together on a couch for a *tête-à-tête* and furniture had to be widened to accommodate the extra width of the skirt. Visits to the theatre or opera proved expensive since it was necessary to buy tickets for the seats on either side. The French queen herself,

By the 1750s the panniers measured as much
as 3 m (9¾ ft) from side to side and created
a host of practical problems.

Une Boulangére.   *Eine Beckhin.*

en forme de brioche. 1. eine Semel. 2. une couronne. 2. ein Cranz. 3. un bout en bras. 3. Ringel
iquelin. 4. eine Brezen. 5. un pain blanc. 5. ein Weckhen. 6. du pain bis. 6. Roggen od. schwarz Br
ain blanc. 7. weiß Brod. 8. brioche. 8. Eyer Zöpffel. 9. pain d'anis. 9. Anis Brod. 10. 11. pain de sr
9. 11. Haus Brod. 12. poußetter. 12. ein Brainwisch. 13. corbeil. 13. Körbe. 14. vendre le pain
                                     Brod verknissen.
nqelbrecht fecit.   Cum Priv. Maj.   M. Engelbrecht e.vixd.

Superfluity of Ornaments

The appearance of the panniers provoked wry comment
in the pages of Addison and Steele's *Spectator*, where every
aspect of fashionable society was scrutinised. 'The fair sex
are run into great extravagances. Their petticoats are now
blown up into a most enormous concave...the Superfluity
of Ornaments...seem to have fallen from their heads
upon their lower parts. What they have lost in Height
they have made up in Breadth and contrary to all rules
of Architecture widen their foundations at the same
time as they shorten the Super structure.'

Above: An eighteenth-century engraving demonstrates
the practical origins of the pannier.

Right: The Infanta Magarita of Austria, daughter of
Philip IV of Spain, dressed as a miniature adult.

Opposite: An engraving for a costume design for a Fury
in Jean-Philippe Rameau's *Hippolyte et Aricie*.

while ably demonstrating her high
status and attracting admiring glances,
was forced to sidle rather inelegantly
sideways through a door.

Although the fame and popularity of
Parisian dressmakers were destined
to grow, the French Revolution put a
peremptory end to both Queen Marie
Antoinette and her ostentatious style.
The elaborate drapery and width of the
panniers was replaced with a simplicity
of dress from which all traces of the
decadence and extravagance of the
Court of Versailles were firmly removed.

By the eighteenth century the mantua or overgown was a formal costume worn at court. This English mantua, of heavily embroidered silk featuring silver thread, was made in the 1740s.

Even a heavy-set woman, with her flesh displaced by tightly laced stays and hidden by the

absurdly wide pannier skirt, could look small-waisted and delicate within her embroidered carapace.

Crinolines

In the 1830s, Queen Victoria of England presided over a fashion that saw women of every class adopting the most impractical means to spread their skirts, apparently prepared to risk life and limb to achieve the desired effect. In its original form, the crinoline was a stiffened petticoat made from linen and horsehair taking its name from the French word *crin* for horsehair and *lin* for linen. As time went on, more petticoats were used to pad the skirt until eventually six were considered absolutely essential. So it is hardly surprising that Victorian ladies suffered attacks of the vapours, particularly on hot summer days, when the weight of the horsehair petticoats became unbearable.

Decorative Cage

The introduction of the cage crinoline in the 1850s served to release women from the horrors of their horsehair padding. Patented by an American, W. S. Thomas, it proved a huge success and meant that, at last, women could freely move their legs beneath their skirts. Although it was still called a crinoline, the cage version was actually a skirt stretched over a series of hoops made of springy steel, linked with lace and ribbons, increasing in diameter as they approached the floor.

Women were delighted – they could sit without creasing their ball gowns and walk with a graceful swinging motion, which afforded their admirers the glimpse of a shapely ankle. When the wind blew, however, the crinoline lifted alarmingly and made the wearing of long drawers an absolute must.

Steel Industry Boom

Although it might seem to our eyes as if women were being trapped inside a metal cage, at the time the steel hoop of the cage crinoline was considered liberating. It was the first fashion to be truly democratic in that it was adopted by all classes, although the quality of the cheaper versions meant rather unattractive steel ridges were visible through the outer skirt.

It certainly provided extra jobs for the steel industry and, at the height of its

There were obvious hazards connected with the wearing of the cage crinoline. Passers-by could be knocked off the pavement by a flailing skirt and a room filled with Victorian bric-a-brac cleared in a twinkling.

Top: This sequence from a satirical cartoon, *The Reign of the Crinoline*, lampoons the surreal absurdity of the crinoline. As the eighteenth-century philosopher Jean-Jacques Rousseau said of the women of his time: 'Everything depends on her...nothing is done except by her or for her'.

Left: The crinoline created a 'zone of exclusion' for young unmarried women, keeping any suitors literally at arm's length.

Above: For day wear, women of the Victorian era dressed like mobile wedding cakes, in crinolines with pagoda- or bell-shaped sleeves and high necks, adorned with flounces, frills, ribbon and lace.

Opposite: A young woman is fitted for a party dress of moderate width (top), while another adopts a modest pose as her escort orders the gate opened (bottom). Clearly, her crinoline won't fit through the turnstile.

28   shape shifting

Take what precautions we may against fire, so long as the hoop is worn, life is never safe.

London's *The Illustrated News of the World*, 1863

popularity in 1860, enough steel was produced in Sheffield to make half a million hoops in one week. Crinoline-making became an important industry, helping to standardise the appearance of the fashionable woman in the last decades of the century.

The Hazards of Hoops

There were obvious hazards connected with the wearing of the cage crinoline. Passers-by could be knocked off the pavement by a flailing skirt, and a room filled with Victorian bric-a-brac cleared in a twinkling. Women were better able to negotiate doors and gates but if they tripped and fell they were helpless, their long drawers exposed for all to see. In factories the impractical gown caught in machines, and on farms girls soaked up cartloads of mud as they tramped across the fields.

Sitting down with any decorum required careful planning, and furniture was adapted to suit the dress. Chairs were made with short legs and seats that sloped back to accommodate the bulging skirt. But more horrifying was the fact that the light material covering the steel hoops was highly flammable. In one terrible incident in Santiago in 1863, fire swept through a church, trapping the female members of the congregation, who were immobilised not just by panic but also by their blazing skirts.

But the cage crinoline was rapidly falling out of fashion as the interest of the dress now shifted to the rear.

Women were to be released from their cage but were also destined to concentrate on a part of their anatomy that Queen Victoria seemed to feel required layers of extra padding that was intended to emphasise and exaggerate their bottoms instead – a rather doubtful forward step in the fight for women's liberation (see page 32.)

Circle Skirts

After the end of World War II, the love of big skirts found its expression in the fashion for huge circle skirts, cut from a single piece of fabric with a hole in the middle. In what was perhaps a response to the austerity of the war years and the rationing of material, Christian Dior's version cast a glance back at the Victorian style of the 1890s, when skirts were also cut from one piece of material but with a ruffle added to give length. In its 1950s incarnation, the circle skirt was calf-length, nipped in at the waist and supported by a stiff crinoline petticoat.

Poodle Skirt

The 'poodle skirt', which originated in the United States, was the teenage version of the circle skirt and soon all the rage. Made out of felt in bold, vibrant colours, it was the perfect outfit for the rock'n'roll era, flaring up with every wild dance turn to reveal the petticoats beneath.

The name came from the fact that the first skirts had literally been appliquéd with cutouts of poodles, but they were soon to become the 'palette' on which teenage girls could express their personality. To the sequins, beads and embroidery that covered their surfaces were added appliqués of anything from telephones to black vinyl records screaming 'See You Later Alligator'.

A fashion that had once seen women caged and constricted by metal hoops was transformed into a style that these girls, for the first time in history, made all their own.

Above: Dior's New Look required a tiny waist achieved by a boned and back-laced corset called a 'waspy'. Givenchy's interpretation pairs a lacquer-printed skirt with a quilted satin jacket.

The Launch of the Modern Crinoline

The crinoline was to make a brief reappearance in the 1930s when leading designers such as Balenciaga and Molyneux attempted to break away from the rather austere line of the tailored clothes of the pre-war era. An enthusiastic caption in a 1938 *Vogue* greeted it with enthusiasm: 'Crinolines bring to the London scene the ample sweep and porcelain femininity of an earlier age. Once more you sail, brave as a full-rigged ship.' In the early 1950s, Fath created lavish ballgowns, worthy of *Gone with the Wind* (see opposite), for stylish young Parisennes.

Bustles

In the 1870s, the crinoline began to shrink in size and Victorian women escaped their hooped cage – only to find themselves constrained by narrow skirts with a huge bump at the back. This was to be the notorious bustle, which grew to such a size that a tray complete with teapot and teacups might be safely perched upon it.

Backlash

The bustle first started to appear in order to counteract the droop at the back of a woman's skirt, caused by the heavy swathe of material draped over a crinoline. Women still needed some form of artifice to make their waists look smaller and, besides, by the late 1860s the classic bell-like shape of the crinoline had evolved into a flatter shape at the back and sides, with the fabric gathered at the back. Gathering fabric over a bustle at the back of the dress was a way of incorporating both movement and shape.

Polonaise Bustles

The robe *à la polonaise* or polonaise appeared in the 1770s and 1780s, and was revived about a century later. Basically it was an overskirt with a fitted bodice that was cut away and gathered at the back to reveal an underskirt at the front, typically in a contrasting colour or fabric. It probably derived from the necessity for a woman to somehow haul her voluminous skirts out of the mud when she was outdoors. In the late nineteenth century, various styles were fashionable in both England and France.

The term 'polonaise' was still being used in the mid-twentieth century to describe any kind of drapery around the skirt.

Exaggerated Erotic Shape

By the 1880s, the shape of the bustle protruding behind the dress perfectly balanced the wearer's bust, creating

Above left: A polonaise of rose silk and silver gauze.

Left: *Punch* magazine's gastropod version of the bustle.

The shape of the bustle protruding behind the dress perfectly balanced the wearer's bust.

Left: A wire cage, comprising a series of hoops attached by straps to a waist band, provided the scaffolding for the bustle.

an exaggerated shape that even the most buttoned-down Victorian men found appealingly erotic.

The change from the characteristic bell shape of the crinoline was subtle at first, with the front being flattened, the surplus fabric swept back and the dress pulled into shape with tapes and buttons. A separate bustle, made of horsehair, was worn over the crinoline, and by 1870 the crinoline was discarded altogether in favour of the bustle.

All the fabric was gathered at the back and a narrow fanned train fell from the shoulders. At first the bustle appeared only on ballgowns, but it soon became a feature of day dresses.

The bustle meant that the father of haute couture, English fashion designer Charles Frederick Worth, could keep his textile suppliers in business, for what the skirt lacked in fullness at the front it made up for in the extremely generous drapery at the back. A slender figure was desirable if the wearer was to carry off the narrow skirt and flattened bodice and, while the bustle survived, the slender look was short-lived. Certainly it would have done little to flatter the rather roly poly contours of Queen Victoria of England in her later years.

Left: Walking up a flight of stairs would have been rendered almost impossible by this knee-high sash, called a fetter, which was later teamed with a hobble skirt (see page 57). We can only assume it was added to heighten the effect of the bustle and train.

An even more exaggerated shape of bustle appeared in the 1880s. Straw-filled cushions were sewn into the skirt and a series of half hoops inserted into the lining so it was thrown out horizontally from waist level behind.

Left: Renoir's 1874 portrait of *La Parisienne*, known as 'The Blue Lady'. New technology had made it possible to manufacture blue-dyed fabric, once a luxury afforded only by the rich.

Functional sewing machines and synthetic dyes began to appear by the mid-nineteenth century, reducing the cost of making clothes. Dressmaking became 'democratised' and, once clothes could be bought 'off the peg', people on modest incomes could attempt to copy the fashionable *beau monde*.

The Rise and Fall of the Derrière

An even more exaggerated shape of bustle appeared in the 1880s. Straw-filled cushions were sewn into the skirt and a series of half hoops inserted into the lining so it was thrown out horizontally from waist level behind. A decade later, however, the bustle had shrunk until it was only a pad and the distinctive shape of Edwardian fashion emerged.

Above: Both the bust and the bustle are depicted as promontories in a French daily newspaper.

Below: Young German ladies wear ballgowns with trains and overskirts draped like Austrian blinds.

For all the trimming with lace and ribbons and fringes, bustles remain a rather comic footnote in fashion history. Together with the long trains that often accompanied them, they still make a rare appearance on the red carpet but there seems little chance that women would revisit a shape that exaggerated the size of their derrières.

Victorian Dress Reform

In the latter half of the nineteenth century, suffragettes on both sides of the Atlantic were starting to campaign for the vote as well as more sensible clothing for women – clothing that would allow them some physcial freedom. The bustle not only impeded movement but also constituted a heavy weight that had to be supported from the waist alone.

Trains

In the nineteenth century a flowing train was sometimes added to the bustle to help achieve the all-important grand entrance. Of course, sweeping the floor meant the elegant train soon looked rather the worse for wear, so a diligent courtier would scurry to tie it up into the bustle once the attention-grabbing moment was past.

Above left: In the fifteenth century, Isabella of Bavaria required two ladies-in-waiting to handle her train.

Left: A society bride photographed in London, in 1920. Her satin and lace wedding dress is based on the fashion of the day, with her cloche-style veil and train the main concessions to the occasion.

Trailing Behind

Court trains had always been a fashionable means of giving a dress an all-important makeover and, by extending it by about 30 cm (1 ft), transforming it into a sumptuous gown fit for royal balls. It was this short 'sweep train' that was also in vogue in the late nineteenth century while more elaborate trains were displayed in the chapel and cathedral gowns associated with weddings.

Above: In Jean Beraud's *La Soirée* (1878), the women wear gowns with cathedral trains.

Right: Marie Louise, Empress of the French and Napoleon Bonaparte's second wife, wears a brocade gown with a cathedral train.

The chapel train was a 'modest' 1 m (3 ft) long while the much longer cathedral train could only be worn by members of the royal court. In 1981, Princess Diana's famous wedding dress boasted a train that was an extraordinary 8 m (26¼ ft) long and almost prevented her father from sitting beside her in the glass coach.

These days trains make the odd rare appearance, mainly at society weddings and on Hollywood's red carpet.

The Rococo Interpretation

The Watteau train was named after the eighteenth-century French artist whose paintings featured society women wearing trains falling elegantly from the shoulder. This style is quite popular for wedding dresses today.

Draping & Winding

To the ancient Greeks and Romans, the ability to get dressed by winding a simple rectangle of cloth of various sizes around their bodies was a sure sign of an advanced civilisation. In the eyes of the Romans at least, tailored clothes were barbaric and at one period in their history they even decreed the death penalty for anyone who had the temerity to be caught wearing them.

Swaddling Clothes

Both men and women wore the *chiton*, a long length of fabric draped over the shoulder and secured by a fibula, an ornate form of safety pin. The Roman *stola*, the rather humble female equivalent of the male *toga*, was worn by married women. A long, sleeveless tunic made of cotton, wool or silk, it was suspended from the shoulders by short straps and a girdle wound under the breast to create broad folds above.

A less than flattering garment, the *stola* was covered by a long cloak called a *palla*, which was draped over the left shoulder, under the right arm, back across the body then thrown over the left arm when it was time to venture outdoors. With the Roman matron swaddled in so many layers, her husband must have been confident her modesty would be preserved. One over-zealous husband, however, divorced his wife for absentmindedly stepping out with her head uncovered.

A Lethal Weapon

While the clothes worn by Roman and Athenian woman were simple, their colour and the ornaments, and girdles that held them in place, broadcast a clear message about status. The *chiton* was often richly coloured in glowing red, deep purple or vivid saffron, but the version worn by the poor was uniformly plain and drab.

The girdles might be made of gold, and the fibula that held the draped

Above left: Bronze and enamel, bird-shaped fibula from imperial Rome, 27 BC–476 AD.

Left: In this Roman mosaic from the first century BC, Plato converses with his disciples. The men show how versatile a garment the *chiton* was.

With the Roman matron swaddled in so many layers, her husband must have been confident her modesty would be preserved.

A timeless classic – Fortuny's Delphos dress, in pleated apricot silk, 1912. All the hand-pleated dresses were dyed using traditional methods and materials.

garments in place grew in size and could even be used as a weapon should the wearer ever need to ward off unwelcome advances.

Modern Drapery

In 1912, inspired by classical Greek drapery, the Spanish designer Mariano Fortuny created the Delphos dress, a shift in finely pleated silk, weighted with hand-blown Murano glass beads to accentuate a woman's curves. These dresses are considered works of art.

In contemporary times, draping was shown at its most effective by the Parisienne designer, Madame Gres, whose draped and pleated gowns were famous for their simplicity. In her 1970s exhibition she moved from Grecian simplicity to bolder avant-garde designs, making the same neoclassical gown in a dazzling range of styles.

The Long & the Short of It

The revolutionary mini and micro-mini of the mid-twentieth century both had an unexpected medieval precedent – the cotehardie, a sort of mini tunic for men. Unlike the micro-mini, however, it eventually failed to cover even the wearer's genitals, attracting the attention of both clergy and law-makers.

Medieval Men's Mini

While in medieval times women's dresses demurely skimmed the ankle, men's hems went up and down with exciting rapidity. As tailors began to shape clothing with curved seams to accentuate the natural contours of the body, a sleeker, more youthful silhouette became the fashion and the *cotehardie*, which fitted like a second skin, began to replace the looser tunic. Male courtiers with a tendency to corpulence were forced to resist that second helping of roast hog as they buttoned and laced themselves in. A shapely leg was important too, for this new version of the tunic barely reached the knees.

Immodest Measures

While this mini length may have been practical for military clothing at a time when a long gown would have impeded movement, devoted followers of fashion allowed the tunic to work its way up their thighs!

As the cotehardie became skimpier and more close-fitting, its 'immodesty' drew barbed comments from clerics. A disapproving French chronicler wrote that 'men, in particular noblemen, took to wearing tunics so short and tight they reveal what modesty bids us hide'. The law soon went into action, and those deemed to be making an exhibition of themselves were forced to lower their hemline a vital few centimetres.

Miniskirt

A small, unpretentious piece of fabric was to become the fashion story of the 1960s, providing teenage girls – forced for so long to dress like their mothers – with a provocative style of their own. The miniskirt, however, can boast some very ancient predecessors.

Archaeologists have discovered figurines dating back to 5400 BC wearing what looks remarkably like the 1960s miniskirt. In the caves of our Stone Age ancestors are drawings

A disapproving French chronicler wrote that 'men, in particular noblemen, took to wearing tunics so short and tight they reveal what modesty bids us hide'.

of what is called the 'string skirt', one of the most provocative short skirts of all time. In ancient Egypt, a fresco shows a female dancer disporting herself in a revealing miniskirt. The ancient Greeks and Romans, on the other hand, favoured the short tunic for military wear only.

Mary Quant, who opened her boutique 'Bazaar' on the King's Road in London in 1955, is mainly credited with producing the 1960s version of this skimpy garment. With her finger firmly on the pulse of street fashion, she began to provide a youthful alternative to Parisienne haute couture. Thought to be named after Quant's favourite car, the mini became an instant hit and from 1961 hemlines were on the rise. Five years later, in spite of much head-shaking from an older generation, hems had reached the upper thighs.

The 'Swinging Sixties' were at their height in every sense and London, rocking to the music of The Beatles and The Rolling Stones, revelled in being the leader of a fashion that focused exclusively on youth.

Above: The men in this fifteenth-century illustration are wearing the close-fitting cotehardie, which barely skimmed their hips.

Left: Sixties fashion, epitomised by bright block colours and short hemlines. Famous British model Twiggy is in the pink outfit.

Opposite: A fashionable outfit for French men in the early fifteenth century, featuring the cotehardie.

shape shifting   41

In 1964 French designer André Courrèges introduced his Moon Girl collection in France. The show-stopper was the space-age mini dress with 'astronaut' hats and goggles.

A New Freedom

The classlessness of the mini was perfectly in tune with the *zeitgeist* of the age, as traditional values were challenged and young women sought to escape from the roles of stay-at-home wife and mother that had previously defined them. The arrival of the contraceptive pill seemed to complete the revolution and they felt ready to stride confidently into the future, independent career girls at ease with their own sexuality.

Stockings and suspenders, which had restricted the length of their skirts, were discarded in favour of the freedom offered by brightly coloured tights. Wet-look PVC, easy-care acrylic and polyester were the new fashion materials in mind-blowing Op Art- and Pop Art-influenced designs. (See Spaced Out, page 146.)

It was liberation indeed, but the miniskirt, while it seemed to empower, also represented the vulnerability of the wearer and a risk of exploitation. To carry it off successfully, girls needed to retain the figures of prepubescent schoolgirls. While the image of the waiflike model Twiggy was the one to which they aspired, *Lolita*, Nabokov's fictional teenage temptress, was a disturbing presence on the scene.

Reversal of Roles

The popularity of the miniskirt lasted until the end of the decade. Paco Rabanne upped the ante with his 'body jewellery' collection, designing a plastic

Maxi Skirts

Hemlines were to plummet at the end of the 1960s as the economic and political climate became bleaker, unemployment rose and the conflict in Vietnam cast a long shadow. The appearance of the midi dress, with the hemline skimming the calf, evolved into the longer 'maxi', which reached below the ankle and often trailed dangerously along the ground. Luckily, platform shoes often saved the unwary from disaster.

Above: In the early 1970s, a period of flamboyant self-expression, Twiggy (left) and Pattie Boyd wear maxicoats in bold geometric patterns with broad-brimmed floppy hats.

chainmail miniskirt in 1966 as well as a throwaway minidress to cater for those so anxious to keep up with fashion they were prepared to discard yesterday's clothes! The era marked an extraordinary reversal of roles as mothers also embraced the youth cult. They were seen haunting the trendy boutiques on London's Carnaby Street in search of a miniskirt, desperate to fit into their daughters' clothes.

Anything Goes

By 1972, skirts and dresses became more fluid and romantic as the eagerness for the brave new world of the future was replaced by a love affair with the past. The folkloric influences and the 'flower power' of the Hippy movement found its expression in natural fabric and paisley and flowery designs, intended to allow women to rediscover the 'sacred feminine' side of their natures.

But many still clung to the miniskirt of their youth. Indeed the 1970s was to prove a decade when 'anything goes', preparing the way for a time when individual expression would be valued above conforming to the latest trend.

Hose to Hotpants

Throughout history there have been some unfortunate fashions that flatter only the few. As Mary Quant put it so succinctly in the 1960s, a woman is only as young as her knees. Yet hemlines continue to zoom up and down like yo-yos, one decade revealing an elegant, well-turned ankle, the next unveiling an entire thigh.

Hose

Crusaders, returning to their European homelands, had ensured the opening up of trade routes to the Near East, bringing back with them not only exotic Oriental materials but also new notions of how clothes should be worn. Instead of the long breeches that had often been combined with leg-bandages bound in a criss-cross pattern, hose or stockings now became the popular choice. Cut out of wool or cloth to follow the shape of the leg, these reached just below the knee and were often brightly coloured or patterned.

By the twelfth century hose had risen higher and were made wide enough at the top to be pulled over the breeches, which rapidly shrank, eventually disappearing altogether.

In the fifteenth century men tucked their long shirts into their hose and tied or laced it to their doublet. This left a rather vital area between the two pieces of hose uncovered, so a cloth triangle was hastily laced on to bridge the gap. It became the codpiece (see page 184).

This page (clockwise from left): The elegant Sir Nathaniel Bacon in breeches and hose; sixteenth-century German soldiers; and an example of the 'tottering triangle'.

Opposite: The Three Degrees, an American trio, model their skin-tight flares in a London street in 1974.

Petticoat Breeches

Men's fashions, which had undergone a woefully dismal period as Puritan values were imposed under Oliver Cromwell's Protectorate, took on a fresh lease of life in 1660 with the restoration of Charles II to the English throne. Petticoat breeches, arguably one of the most extraordinary male costumes in history, first appeared at the French court and were now adopted with enthusiasm. The military style of the previous age was replaced by voluminous skirts, caught at the waist and knee by brightly coloured ribbons, and protruding from below a short doublet.

Tottering Triangle

A looser and more elaborate version of petticoat breeches, called 'rhinegrave' after the French count who had introduced the style, soon became even more popular. The silhouette that men presented as they flounced and flaunted their skirts gave rise to what was called 'the tottering triangle'. The one drawback to this picture of sartorial excess was the fact that the wearer of the breeches was forced to tie back his coat tails.

Historians of the age were less than impressed. One commented acidly: 'Taste and elegance were abandoned for extravagance and folly'. Samuel Pepys was to remark wryly in his 1661 diary that the petticoat breeches were so huge it was possible to put both legs in one compartment!

Oxford Bags

In the 1920s, a new informality was apparent in men's dress and, for a brief period, the eccentric 'Oxford bags' became popular. These were extremely wide trousers – 63 cm (2 ft) at the knee and 56 cm (1¾ ft) around the bottom, allowing only the tips of the shoes to be revealed.

One theory traces their origins to the voluminous towelling trousers that undergraduate oarsmen wore over their shorts when they took part in the university boat race. They soon became the fashion in America too, and caricatures appeared of undergraduates on American campuses dancing the Charleston, their vast 'bags' flapping wildly as they gyrated. Although this rather comical style was short-lived, trousers were to remain wide until the end of the 1930s.

Bell-bottoms and Flares

In the nineteenth century, American sailors began to sport a jaunty style of wide-legged trousers, which ended in a bell shape and may have seemed appropriate apparel for keeping one's balance on deck. But by what seems an amazing leap, bell-bottoms, as they were known, were to become a 'hot' fashion for women in the 1960s. This new version flared out at the back and front from the calf down and ended in

No self-respecting rock star would strut their stuff without a swish of flaring, flapping denim around their knees.

Harem pants became popular again in the 1980s when the wide ballooning legs, tight at the ankle and with a long crotch, were fully visible.

Model Rene Russo wearing silk harem pants, 1976.

a slightly curved hem that could be 46 cm (1½ ft) in circumference. By the end of the 1960s, the Hippy movement had adopted the style, and denim bell-bottoms were soon making their appearance at rock festivals and on sidewalks, the trailing hems soaking up the mud.

It was in the early 1970s that trouser hems became even wider and 'flares' often replaced the slightly more moderate bell-bottoms. These were tight around the thigh and looked as if the wearer had skirts attached to their knees – the material was cut so that it spread at the bottom as much as 66 cm (2¼ ft). Bell-bottoms had evolved from high fashion designed by Ralph Lauren, who had made stylish tailored trouser suits for women, to being the recognised 'uniform' of the Hippy movement. No self-respecting rock star would strut their stuff without a swish of flaring, flapping denim around their knees.

Harem Pants

Influenced by Eastern art and performances given by the Russian ballet, the French couturier Paul Poiret created a storm in 1910 with his flamboyant and enormously theatrical 'harem' pants. Made from rich silks in vibrant, glowing colours, these appeared beneath the hems of women's skirts, their softly draped style in sharp contrast to the rigid shapes which had been favoured before.

But only the keenest followers of fashion ventured out in the exotic 'Poiret pants', which attracted caustic comments from their suffragette contemporaries. To these reformers, wearing a costume better suited to a slave in an oriental harem seemed less than helpful to their cause.

Harem pants became popular again in the 1980s when the wide ballooning legs, tight at the ankle and with a long crotch, were fully visible.

Hot Pants

As the miniskirt began to fall out of vogue, tiny shorts, often made of satin and designed to accentuate a woman's buttocks and legs, offered an alternative to the maxi's folds. Known as 'hot pants', these ultra-short shorts with an inside seam that was sometimes just 5 cm (2 in) long, were often worn with bibs, straps and long white socks or boots, which seemed to emphasise, a shade uncomfortably, a sexy schoolgirl image. However, some men were brave enough to be hot-panted, too.

The fad soon faded as the escapees from the mini finally succumbed to the all-concealing maxi length and demoted their hot pants, reluctantly, to the back of the wardrobe.

Shoulders & Sleeves

When fashion designers become weary of raising and lowering hemlines, or of manipulating the human torso to make it look fat, thin or just misshapen, they turn their attention to the shoulders and, in particular, sleeves – slashed and embroidered, puffed and sheer, or even resembling a large leg of lamb.

Japanese Long Sleeves

The traditional Japanese costume, the kimono, worn at one time by both women and men, and made out of delicately embroidered or hand-painted silk, is characterised by long flowing sleeves. Originally adapted from China in the fifth century, it became the costume worn by women alone in the nineteenth century. Traditionally, unmarried girls wore a style called a furisode, with long 'swinging sleeves' that touched the floor when they let their arms drop to their sides.

The Sleeves That Talk

The hugely valuable kimonos worn by the geishas or 'artistic entertainers', who have retained their mystery for centuries behind the bamboo screens of Japanese tea houses, also wore long sleeves.

These took on a symbolic importance whenever the geisha entertained. A glimpse of the wrist as the sleeve fell back a fraction during the traditional tea-making ceremony could seem infinitely suggestive, although her feelings would remain hidden behind the expressionless white mask of her face. Her long sleeves were also used to symbolically dab away tears – again, another carefully staged movement in her extensive artistic repertoire.

Big Shoulders

The desire of European men to exhibit their power and masculinity in the early sixteenth century meant a geometric shape was favoured, with exaggerated broad shoulders tapering to a very prominent codpiece (see page 184).

Above left: Japanese Kabuki dancer, 1758.

Right: Hans Holbein the Younger portrait of an imposing Henry VIII of England.

The desire of European men to exhibit their power and masculinity in the early sixteenth century meant a geometric shape was favoured, with exaggerated broad shoulders.

…clothes became layered and more voluminous, with full sleeves – slashed to reveal a chemise or shirt beneath…

The doublet, a tight-fitting buttoned jacket, emphasised the width of the padded shoulders, and the sleeves were of a different coloured material and design to emphasise the triangular shape. It was a style that was mainly adopted by the nobility – no doubt intended to give even the puniest a swaggering presence in the back-stabbing and competitive atmosphere of the English Tudor court.

Slashed Sleeves

As the weather in Western Europe cooled during the Little Ice Age of 1550 to 1850, clothes became layered and more voluminous, with full sleeves – slashed to reveal a chemise or shirt beneath – the focus of attention. The fashion lasted well into the next century, when a ribbon above the elbow helped gather the sleeve, known as the virago, into two puffs.

Elaborate slashing was particularly popular in Germany, where garments might be assembled from alternating bands of contrasting fabrics.

Huge Sleeves

In the 1830s, the small puffed sleeves popular in the early decades of the century expanded into ballooning shapes, gathered tightly into the wrist. Once again fashion was looking back to

shaped until it was bound in at the wrist, resembling at its fullest an elephant's ear. It was an era when the costume of the upper classes ensured that all useful activity – other than raising a porcelain teacup to the lips – could be successfully avoided.

Shoulder Pads

The 1980s saw a return to the wide shoulder look, but this time it was adopted by women, determined to establish their presence in the workplace by attaching wider and wider pads to the Velcro lining the shoulder seams of their suits. The silhouette was unashamedly mannish, but it was infused with glamour as career women made it their own, now feeling confident in boardrooms where men were soon struggling to compete.

an earlier age, revisiting the dolman sleeves worn in the Middle Ages but originally seen in Turkey and other parts of the Middle East. The dolman, a loose cape-like robe, had loose sleeves formed from the folds of the robe's fabric. The ease with which the sleeve could be sewn in proved an attraction, and it was adopted by Europeans in the sixteenth century.

Leg-of-mutton Sleeves

In the first decades of the twentieth century, the fascination with designs from the East meant people were eager to rediscover such styles. Leg-of-mutton sleeves, which followed the shape of the dolman, were wide at the armhole but tapered towards the wrist. Sometimes they were cleverly cut so they were of a piece with the garment.

Also making a brief appearance in the 1830s was the aptly named elephant sleeve, in which the material was not

Wandering Waistlines

Fashion often dictates a look or shape that tends to disregard the shape of the human body, sometimes exaggerating a natural curve, or striving to eliminate it completely, often with the assistance of highly engineered under- and overgarments.

The 'Pregnant' Look

When knights returned to Europe from their crusading campaigns in the Holy Lands in the twelfth and thirteenth centuries, they brought with them fresh notions of beauty and style, together with high expectations of the ladies waiting for them in castles across the land. They were eager for their patient spouses to adopt a sensuous, graceful, feminine style that would express their appreciation for such manly virtues.

With barely a raised eyebrow, the women of Europe complied, and a high waistline was used to accentuate the new femininity. The 'pregnant' look, popular in the fourteenth century, seemed to signify a fecundity that complimented the virility of the crusading knights. With stomachs protruding and hips flared, women waddled as if they were pregnant with a phantom child.

Peascod

Elizabeth I of England was to influence men's fashion at court just as surely as she dictated the style worn by her ladies. The bulky, masculine silhouette popular in the time of Henry VIII was replaced by a more feminine shape as men too were constrained by corsets and wore a curious full-stomached doublet filled with padding called a peascod, shaped to make the belly protrude as if they too were pregnant.

To add to this extraordinary effect, broad-hipped breeches, known as melons, swelled out beneath. The queen seemed determined that the male of the species should suffer for

Above left: In this 1955 studio portrait, the American actress Jane Russell celebrates her curves in a shoulderless dress.

Above: Sir Philip Sidney, the English poet, courtier and soldier, wears a peascod in this contemporary portrait.

Right: In this painting by Botticelli we see women sporting the 'pregnant look', which was popular in the fourteenth century.

fashion just as she did, although he might have counted himself lucky to be encased in a peascod rather than a wheel farthingale!

No Bending

Elizabethan bodices, stiffened with buckram or even wood, meant any foolhardy attempt to bend was defeated by a sharp jab in the ribs. Waists were so rigidly squeezed by these outer corsets that inner organs were often displaced (see page 179).

Ancient Precursor to the Polonaise

The clothes worn in Crete before the collapse of the Minoan civilisation seem strangely to anticipate the polonaise look of the 1870s, with high, nipped-in waists and flounces reaching to the ground (see page 32). Bare breasts, however, were 'framed' by the costume, which had tight sleeves to the elbow, and would certainly have caused apoplexy on the nineteenth century fashion scene.

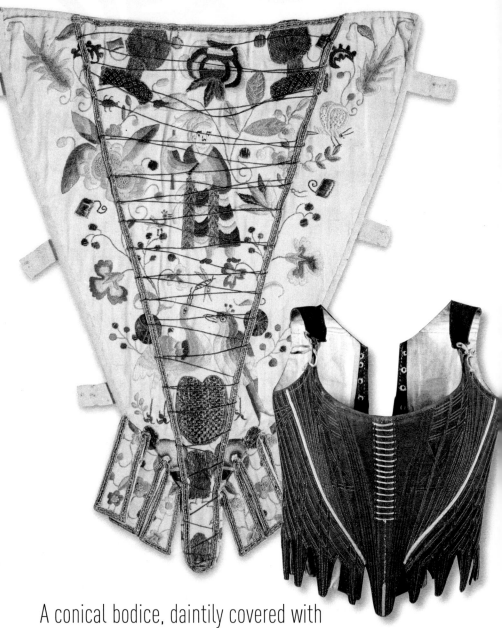

Stays

During the seventeenth and eighteenth centuries, the war on waists continued. A conical bodice, daintily covered with damask or linen, performed the Herculean task of pushing the waistline further down by means of the rigid stays with which they were stiffened. Often made of whalebone or wood, the stays acted as additional weapons to assist the squeezing apparatus of the corset. Both movement and breathing were impeded and the long-suffering fashion victim often succumbed to fainting fits as she gasped for air.

Not surprisingly, the term 'straight-laced' found its way into the language.

Stomacher

During the late sixteenth century, voluminous skirts effectively concealed a woman's lower body but the midriff continued to be cruelly clamped. It was pinched by a stiffened external corset shaped like a triangle. Appropriately called a stomacher, it extended down to ensure that it too was firmly contained. In contemporary portraits of society ladies wearing this low, narrow waistline, we can detect a look of pained stoicism on their white faces.

A conical bodice, daintily covered with damask or linen, performed the Herculean task of pushing the waistline further down...

Celebrating Curves

Stone Age women were much admired for their generous folds of flesh, thought to indicate they were well fed and fertile. At a time when there was no guarantee of dinner appearing each night, 'big' was certainly equated with 'beautiful', and artefacts show that prominent buttocks were considered ideal. Through the centuries this curvaceous body shape, celebrated by the painter Rubens's rosy, voluptuous nudes in the sixteenth century, was associated with the upper classes, who could afford plenty of food amid a life of leisure. To be thin was to be apparently malnourished, and therefore poor.

It was not until the twentieth century that one of Dorothy Parker's famous aphorisms – 'You can never be too thin or too rich' – began to seem all too apt as women learnt to relentlessly diet and exercise until they achieved the straight-up-and-down shape of the 1920s 'flapper'.

After World War II, when strict rationing came to an end, a voluptuous, fuller figure – epitomised by Marilyn Monroe's curves – was once again admired. But by the 1960s an androgynous waif-like figure was suddenly in vogue, and in recent decades curves have been banished in favour of the lean and hungry look.

the 'S' curve

As the Edwardian era progressed, the shape of the reform corset became more exaggerated. Women still coveted a small waist so the busk (the rigid front of the corset) became heavier, and superfluous flesh was pushed down to the hips. This new corset forced the stomach to slant inwards at the waist, so the bust would overhang more obviously, producing the characteristic 'S' silhouette of the early 1900s. The shape was often further enhanced by wearing lace at the bust-line or lacy blouses to thrust the bust forwards. Never before had corset-cutting and shaping been such a complex job. The corset was now made up of myriad curved pieces, possibly as many as ten to fifteen on each side, as well as gussets, all engineered with whalebone and steel. The more expensive corsets were made from satin or silk and trimmed with lace and ribbon bows, the most popular colour being 'butterfly blue'. The years 1904–1905 were the peak period of the S-curve, and after that time the body line slowly started to straighten up, achieving a new long-line look in about 1907.

Straight Up & Down

A simpler silhouette in women's fashions can sometimes
be linked to social revolution, war and emancipation.
After the crippling extravagance of Marie Antoinette
was cut short by the guillotine during the French
Revolution, it became expedient for women to wear
the Empire line dress, which harkened back to the
loose-fitting garments of ancient times.

The 'hobble' is the latest freak in women's fashions. Skirts are so tight around the ankle that locomotion is seriously impeded and speed is impossible. *New York Times*, 1910

Chilly Empire Line

In the eighteenth century, after the excesses and turmoil of the French Revolution, women were able to discard the stays that had seemed a mark of aristocratic indolence and opt for what were known as Empire line dresses. The waistline moved up to just below the bust and the gown fell straight to the ankle, merely skimming the rest of of their curves.

There were disadvantages to this fashion, for the dress was like a flimsy nightdress with hardly enough material to keep the wearer warm in winter. It also boasted a décolleté neckline for both day and evening wear. Women's fashions of the time seemed to have been designed for a tropical climate, so shawls soon became an essential part of the fashionable lady's wardrobe as she struggled to ward off pneumonia. The Empire silhouette made an encore appearance just before World War I, but the outbreak of hostilities put an end to such an impractical style.

Hobble Skirts

The Edwardian era saw the introduction of the hobble skirt, so narrow at the hem that it became impossible for a woman to take a step of more than 5 to 8 cm (2 to 3 in). An extraordinary development was the 'fetter', made of braid and intended to prevent the skirt from splitting, should a woman take a

Above left: Pale – often white – flimsy fabrics were typical of the Empire line dress. They denoted status, as you probably needed a servant to wash them frequently.

Left: An Empire line robe designed by Paul Poiret, whose innovations included the hobble skirt and the bell-shaped 'lampshade' tunic.

Right: Stage actress Ina Claire in a hobble skirt, 1913.

reckless stride towards mobility and independence (see page 33). In the era of the suffragette movement it seems sadly ironic that, in terms of fashion, women were going backwards, mincing along with tiny steps. Flight from a pursuer – or, indeed, any kind of rapid movement – was impossible.

In the 1960s the long, narrow skirt reappeared in a less exaggerated form, and was often teamed with a twinset, pearls and a pair of killer stilettos (see page 67).

Flatter Flappers

Women had discovered to their surprise that, while the men were away fighting on the frontline, they were able to successfully replace them in their civilian roles. In the 1920s they were determined to show off this new equality by emphasising a boyish silhouette – the 'flapper look'. Their curves disappeared as they cut their hair short and flattened their chests in bold defiance of the conditioning that had kept them in their place for centuries.

Androgynous, Anorexic Look

In the 1930s, androgynous style was perfected by the Hollywood actresses Katharine Hepburn and Marlene Dietrich, who helped to popularise pants for women. Dietrich exuded an understated glamour while wearing mannish suits and hats (see page 143).

Three decades later, the 'flapper look' was reinvented when the English model Twiggy took the fashion world by storm with her waif-like boyish figure, gamin haircut and enormous eyes. In the years that followed, teenage girls became increasingly uncomfortable with a natural, healthy body image that does not conform to the current ideal – too often represented on the catwalks by anorexic models, for whom Size Zero seems the ultimate goal.

Above: Spectacularly thin British model Twiggy, 1966.

Left: Tight-fitting, streamlined suits by French designer Pierre Balmain, 1953.

Far left: The American actress Joan Crawford in a 'flapper' dress, complete with tiers of fringing. The flapper image was strongly associated with 'having a good time' – dancing to jazz, smoking and drinking alcohol, even driving a car.

2
fantastic footwear

If the shoe doesn't fit, must we change the foot? GLORIA STEINEM, b.1934

Killer Heels

A high heel enables you to look down on the world while the world looks up to you. It proves you're well-heeled, and never down-at-heel. It gives an elegant line to the leg and straightens the back. It confers upon the wearer the qualities of dignity, authority, superiority – until, of course, you totter, teeter and tumble.

Above: Dutch wooden clogs, or *klompen*, painted with a traditional pattern. They are still worn today by farmers and gardeners.

The Noble Art of Falling

In the theatres of ancient Greece an audience could tell by a glance at the actor's shoes whether they were in for high drama or low comedy. For tragedy the actors wore a sandal with a built-up cork or wood sole, called a 'buskin' or *cothurnus* – the taller the actor, the more important his role. The gods balanced on 15 or 18 cm (6 or 7 in) of shoe, and would have to be helped down at the end of the performance.

In Japan, a similar shoe, called the *geta*, has been worn for 2000 years to keep the well-shod elevated from the mud and debris of the streets. In Korea they're called *namakshin*, and in India *padukas*, the traditional version often made with high wooden soles.

When Only Wood Would Do

Before the days of smooth-surfaced roads, when most transport involved animals, people needed some sort of footwear that would protect their feet from mud and muck.

For centuries agricultural workers in Europe wore clogs with thick wooden soles as their main shoes. But for those who were used to wearing smart and fashionable shoes as they flirted and chatted indoors, some kind of overshoe was essential for venturing outdoors.

The most common type was the patten, which consisted of a wooden sole raised on two blocks, with a strap to hold it on over the shoe. Variations on the patten were worn by men and women in many countries, and from medieval times up to the twentieth century. Pattens weren't merely functional, however. They could be made with straps in different colours, often had exaggeratedly pointed toes and varied in height.

During the Industrial Revolution, discontented workers would bring production to a halt by chucking a clog, or sabot, into their machines. They became known as saboteurs.

Below: A Japanese man, possibly a Samurai, wears *geta*, thongs on wooden blocks, which would have protected his silk kimono from any dirt, mud, water or snow on the ground.

Below: In this pastel drawing from the eighteenth century, a Turkish woman and her servant both wear pattens. Note the superior elevation of the mistress's pair.

The clog's strength and durability have always made it ideal for farm workers. With no metal to strike sparks, it also became essential footwear for mining or any other industry where there was danger of fire or detonation.

In the early years of the Industrial Revolution in France, discontented workers would bring production to a halt by chucking a clog, or *sabot*, into their machines. They became known as *saboteurs*, and a new word entered the language.

Above: A tasselled
chopine, sheathed
in embroidered fabric
with a lace insert.

Left: A Venetian woman
wears breeches and
chopines, the medieval
inspiration for platform
shoes (see page 67),
under her dress, 1592.

Chopines

The chopine was a patten gone mad.
Developed in fifteenth-century Venice
at the height of that city's domination
as a world power, chopines – worn only
by women – were towering wooden
overshoes that lifted the Venetian
beauty as much as 50 cm (20 in) off the
ground as she tottered through the
narrow streets and across the steep
bridges. Balancing precariously on
these shoes forced the wearer to take
refined and measured steps, with
servants in permanent attendance.

The cork structure was often covered
with kid leather or velvet and decorated
with lace or tassels, but they were
usually hidden out of sight beneath a
long skirt. In England, a man who felt
shortchanged by the discovery, on his
wedding night, that his bride was much
shorter than he'd been led to believe,
was entitled to an annulment.

The fashion lasted for a surprisingly
long time, at one point consuming a
substantial proportion of Spain's cork
production. Some scholars believe
that the very high chopines were
worn almost exclusively by Venice's
prostitutes. The extra height would
enable the women to become walking
advertising hoardings, raised above the
crowds so their wares could be seen.
Other fashion historians claim that
exaggerated chopines were worn by
all the fashionistas of the day, whether
respectable or not. Lower, but still
challenging, chopines continued to be
worn until the seventeenth century.

The Riding Heel and the Splendid Boot

Among shoe historians, there is some
controversy about the origin of the
'proper' heel – where the heel is higher
than the toe. It has been traced back to

Chopines – worn only by women – were towering wooden overshoes that lifted the Venetian beauty as much as 50 cm (20 in) off the ground.

the horsemen of ninth-century Persia, whose high stacked heels helped hold their feet in the stirrups. The idea eventually caught on in Europe, as a feature of specialist boots for men on horses. Not until the sixteenth century did the heel's non-equestrian benefits

Below: In England chopines were called pantobles or mules. This pair, of a relatively moderate height, is made of cork and covered with silk damask. The ribbons helped secure the shoes to the wearer's calves and ankles.

become apparent to the general population, with men wearing high heels before women did.

By the fifteenth century, riding boots were made with an extra piece under the heel to stop the foot from slipping through the stirrup. This 'riding heel' was especially useful while you were out hunting or charging into battle, but had the further advantage of making you look taller when you dismounted.

During the sixteenth and seventeenth centuries, men's boots became major

fashion items – decorated with buckles, fringes and lacing, often with large cuffs turned over at the top, and always with solid, but definitely raised, heels. A fine pair of boots was a necessary part of any swashbuckling musketeer's outfit. King Charles I of England wore boots almost all the time – when he was a child it was thought that he would not be able to walk unaided, but he had special boots made with supports hidden inside the legs to assist his weak, spindly legs.

his red-heeled shoes – his *talons rouges*. A 1673 edict restricted the wearing of *talons rouges* to only the uppermost echelons. For a hundred years or more, red heels could be spotted in the coronation portraits of every royal house of Europe.

The Fall and Rise of Teetering

When Marie Antoinette was taken to the guillotine, she was wearing delicate heeled shoes – the hated symbol of a corrupt and decadent court.

But it wasn't only the revolutionaries who despised the rich folk's fancy shoes. In the American colonies, long before they kicked out the British, the Puritans had passed strict anti-heel laws. 'The poisoned hook', they called it, designed to ensnare a man in a web of lust and sin. In some communities, heel-wearing was considered a sign of a witch (broomstick silhouettes nearly always feature heels).

Left: The Sun King, Louis XIV of France, painted by Hyacinthe Rigaud in 1701, wears a pair of *talons rouges*, their red heels matched by red bows.

Below: The Louis heel, as depicted in a German portfolio of shoe designs.

The Louis Heel

Louis XIV of France was only 1.6 m (5 ft 2 in) in his stockinged feet and very vain. The 'Sun King' often wore a 30-cm (1-ft) wig and 10-cm (4-in) heels. And what heels! Louis's personal shoemaker, Nicholas Lestage, decorated the king's shoes with scenes from his famous battles and designed a more stable heel with a concave curve that spread slightly at the base – still known as the Louis heel. The king's favourites were

A woman wearing stiletto heels exerts more pressure per square centimetre than a three-tonne elephant.

Stilettos

As the twentieth century moved on and the hemline moved up, heels came into their own as symbols of power, sex, sass and style.

Although two world wars tried their best to impose drab, practical, utility footwear on both men and women, at night people dreamed of something better and slighter sexier. In the early 1940s, when Mistinguett, the French cabaret singer, appeared in some ultra-thin tapered heels made for her by the French shoe designer André Perugia, they began to have some inkling of what that might be.

The Italian word *stiletto* means a needle, or a killer's knife. Usually about 7.5 cm (3 in) high, a genuine stiletto has a stem of solid steel or alloy and a diameter of about 1 cm (½ in) at its tip. A woman wearing stiletto heels exerts more pressure per square centimetre than a three-tonne elephant.

The tiny rubber tips of these heels usually wore through quickly, leaving

Above: Two-toned stilletoes, c.1950. Wearing this style of high heel gives definition to the calf muscles and thrusts out the bust and buttocks.

Right: Platform shoes were fashionable in the 1970s. As with many extreme shoe fashions, platforms required a good sense of balance.

a metal point that could do horrendous damage to timber floors, so they were eventually banned from many public buildings. Later stiletto-type heels, with the tip very slightly wider, were made of plastic with a metal core.

The Platform

In the twentieth century men's shoes were comparatively modest and plain, but broke out in a big way during the 1970s. Following fashions set by 'glam rock' musicians as well as top couture designers, trendy young men wore

shoes with heels and increasingly high platform soles. The dominant men's style was a short boot, usually in brightly coloured leather with cut-out or appliqué contrasting designs. Shiny patent leather, sequins and glitter were worn as street- and party-wear.

Platform soles reached 5 cm (2 in) or more, with the square chunky heel adding even more height, and girls wore similar, usually knee-length, boots. For the rest of the century and into the next one, women's fashions occasionally revisited the platform sole.

Pointy Toes

Feet, even in the most attractive of humans, are never pointed. So it's something of a mystery why so many cultures, countries and eras of history have prized long, pointy feet – or at least the appearance of long, pointy feet given by long, pointy shoes. There have been claims, of course, that long, pointy shoes make the feet appear 'dramatic and sexy'. While 'dramatic' can, at a push, be believed, points that extend – as some do – half a metre (20 in) or so would make sexual attraction implausible and actual contact downright dangerous. Nevertheless, here's a look at the irresistible – if unbelievable – rise and rise of pointy shoes.

Above: An elegant young man from 1480, wearing the improbably pointed toe.

Right: The remnants of a pair of men's leather poulaines from the fourteenth or fifteenth century.

Poulaines or Pigaches

In about the twelfth century, the fashion for pointy shoes took Europe by storm. One theory improbably suggests that it all started with a Count Fulk of Anjou who had a deformed foot, but it's far more likely that the style blew in from the East, either with soldiers returning from the Crusades or merchants from the silk roads.

These new-style shoes were called 'poulaines' or 'pigaches'. The points, or poulaines, stuffed with either horsehair or moss, grew until more than half a metre (20 in) was not uncommon. They were curled upwards. They were shaped to look like snakes and fishtails. They had little bells attached.

To avoid tripping over, fashionable young men had to attach cords or chains from the ends of the toes up to garters under their knees. The new way of walking, with the feet raised high and wide to avoid tripping over the shoes, was considered stylish. Suits of armour were made with *sabatons* so long that the wearer couldn't mount or dismount a horse without considerable help, and he couldn't walk at all.

Only men wore the very big points, called 'cracows' – and there are

To avoid tripping over, fashionable young men had to attach cords or chains from the ends of the toes up to garters under their knees.

accounts of young bloods standing on street corners, waggling their shoes suggestively at passing beauties. Just in case the message wasn't clear, the more overt wore pink points.

Laws were passed. A nobleman was entitled to have poulaines that were twice as long as his feet, but a merchant was only allowed to have them the same length. Anyone else could only wear poulaines that were half as long as their feet. A later, more severe law limited the length of all poulaines to 5 cm (2 in) beyond the foot; those who broke the law would be fined and publicly admonished by their local priest, while the shoemaker who had made the offending points would also be fined.

Above: A *khussa*, a traditional Pakistani shoe, hand-crafted with vegetable-tanned leather and strong cotton thread.

Right: Orlando shows off his cracows while conversing with Maugis in *The Garden of Love*, from the Reaud de Montauban cycle, fifteenth century.

Above: In the 1960s winkle-pickers were a requisite part of the sharp-dressing Mod's outfit.

Left: In his London shop, Stan Bartholomew, the creator of the winkle-picker, shows customers just how long the pointy toe could go. The style was inspired by medieval poulaines.

Satan's Claws

This was no nine-day wonder. For nearly 400 years the fever for pointed shoes showed no sign of abating. The Church took a dim view. Not only did these 'Satan's Claws', as they called them, encourage licentiousness, they also made it impossible for the wearers to kneel down in prayer. The Black Plague of 1347, they claimed, was God's punishment on humankind for wearing sinful footwear. In 1367, Pope Urban V banned them outright, threatening wearers with excommunication. Most European countries passed some sort

The Black Plague of 1347, they claimed, was God's punishment on humankind for wearing sinful footwear.

Below: Leopard-print stilettos with a modified pointy toe from the 1960s. In the heyday of the winkle-picker, however, such toes could be several centimetres long.

of sumptuary law limiting shoe length for various classes.

Some accounts reckon it was the six toes of Charles VIII of France that saw off the pointy shoe. To accommodate his polydactylism, he had to wear square toes. The fashion caught on. But since Charles was generally regarded as an idiot, the theory seems unlikely. More likely the world, as it does sometimes, just came spontaneously to its senses.

Winkle-pickers and Roach Kickers

Neither shoe designers nor their customers have ever been happy with a foot-shaped shoe. Although nothing as extreme as the medieval poulaine was seen in Europe for many centuries, every age flirted with its own version of pointiness.

In the 1950s, Italy meant glamour. Italian films, songs, haircuts, suits, dresses and shoes – particularly shoes – became must-haves. The Italian shoe designers began to sharpen their toes – first on women's stilettos, then on men's shoes. In Britain and Australia, they were called 'winkle-pickers',

because they were so sharp you could, metaphorically, use them to pick the flesh out of a periwinkle – a type of tiny shellfish. In the United States they were called, less delicately, 'roach kickers'.

The best were handmade in Italy, two-tone perhaps, or white with black laces, their length emphasised by the ankle-hugging trouser bottoms of the Italian suits with which they were worn. Buckles reappeared, sometimes two on each foot. The ultimate seal of approval came when a winkle-picker version of an elastic-sided, high-ankled boot of a type previously only worn by horse-riders or maiden aunts became the chosen footwear of The Beatles. Rechristened Beatle Boots, for a year or two they became as mandatory for a man of fashion as the black nylon turtle-neck and the hirsute forehead.

Dainty &
Decorative

Buckles and Bows

In the eighteenth century men's shoes were decorated with buckles, which could be very valuable. Even a middle-class man was expected to have solid silver buckles on his shoes, while an aristocrat might well decorate his shoe-buckles with diamonds and other precious stones. The buckles could be attached to different pairs of shoes, of course, but for a man of high fashion, it simply wasn't 'done' to be seen in the same pair of buckles too often.

The heels were usually covered in the same fabric as the shoes – another reason to protect the shoes from mud and dust. Shoes for both men and women were often fastened with silk ribbon. This footwear was designed for socialising indoors, not for going out to earn a living – but then, their wearers didn't have to earn one!

Fashionable eighteenth-century shoes – both men's and women's – were elegant, colourful and designed to be noticed. Many of the smartest were made of fabric – brocade, satin and damask – rather than leather, and were designed to accompany a particular outfit, perhaps in a matching fabric or in colours to tone or contrast with the clothes.

Above: An embroidered shoe with lace, worn by Louis XV, King of France from 1715 until his death in 1774.

Right: A pair of mid-nineteenth-century English shoes for women in striped satin with matching rosettes and elastic ties.

Women's shoes were even more lightweight and frivolous than men's. There's a famous story of a lady in the eighteenth century who complains to her shoemaker that a pair of shoes has fallen apart. The shoemaker looks at her shoes, then responds, a shocked expression on his face: 'But, Madam, you have walked in them!'

Simpering Slippers

During the French Revolution, wearing anything that made you look like a member of the leisured classes could be a serious and even fatal mistake, and consequently clothes became much simpler. The plain styles of this period became fashionable throughout Europe and beyond. Men took to wearing unadorned footwear, often riding boots.

But while women's shoes became simpler than before, and featured low heels, they were still very light and flimsy. A frequently worn style was what we would now call a ballet pump – a plain flat slipper in soft leather. In the early nineteenth century, women also wore sandals, as everything 'Grecian' or 'Classical' was in favour.

3

Ornament
& Ostentation

Fashion is gentility running away from vulgarity and afraid of being overtaken.

WILLIAM HAZLITT, 1778–1830

Over the Top

When image matters, when you need to show the world you're flashier, grander or just plain better than everybody else, the secret is 'dress to impress'. It's a lesson all the top kings and queens, dictators, seducers, bullies and stars have taken to heart. The essential rules are: think big, think shiny, think ruinously expensive, think hopelessly impractical and, if your clothes are solid gold, if they've bankrupted a nation and are so heavy you need a team of burly servants and a forklift just to move off the sofa, you're getting it right.

Above: Unlike other ladies of her time, Marie Antoinette wore breeches when she rode.

The Pearly Queen

Elizabeth I of England was a mistress of PR who knew that image matters. No effort, expense or discomfort was spared in making sure she looked every inch a mighty Queen. Eventually she amassed a collection of an estimated 3000 dresses, each one designed to demonstrate her absolute command. She travelled with 300 carts full of luggage. Those who caught a glimpse of her believed they'd seen a goddess.

In her 1592 portrait by Marcus Gheeraerts the Younger, to symbolise her continuing status as the Virgin

Left: A Chinese silk robe embroidered with 'long-life' characters, c.1870–1911.

Below: In this sixteenth-century portrait by Marcus Gheeraerts the Younger, Elizabeth I wears a creation of extraordinary, almost architectural grandeur, padded to magnify and distort her shape, and framed with lace.

the stitching on a stray jewel from one of her dresses might work loose, fall unnoticed and make their fortune. Not that she could have walked far. These heavy, unwieldy clothes would have made any movement nigh on impossible. But these were never intended to be tennis clothes. They were designed for sitting on a throne and stunning any onlookers into subservience. And they have never been bettered.

The Emperor's New Clothes

During the Qing Dynasty in China, three factories, each with a workforce of hundreds, worked full-time just to turn out clothes for the Imperial family. A robe for the emperor himself could keep a team of 40 embroiderers employed for approximately 2½ years. As well as the usual silk, pearls and precious stones, these sumptuous robes incorporated threads made from the feathers of kingfishers and peacocks, fur of Siberian sable and black fox and even ornaments of fragrant wood.

Traditionally the emperor's robe was decorated with nine dragons. The biggest, on the back, had 'the head of a camel, the horns of a deer, the eyes of a rabbit, the neck of a snake, the claws of an eagle and the paws of a tiger'.

Wedding clothes were always the most extravagant. In 1889, Yehe Nara Jingen married the Emperor Guanxu. A team of embroiderers spent three years covering her wedding gown of dazzling red silk with auspicious symbols and mythical creatures. When Puyi, the last emperor, married Wanrong, acres of red silk were used for wall coverings, carpets and bed hangings. The bridal chamber he described as looking like 'a melted red wax candle'.

Queen, Elizabeth wears white satin and silk covered with a pattern of roses, each one decorated with gold, pearls and precious stones. More pearls are sewn into her wig and great ropes of them hang from her neck to below her waist. Her ruff of fine gauze sits up beyond her ears. She has sprouted 'faerie' wings and she appears to have a ruby the size of an egg shooting out of the back of her headdress. To say she looked like a million dollars would certainly be an understatement.

There are stories of her courtiers following Elizabeth in the hope that

Sequins originated centuries ago in the Mediterranean region. They were small coins that were sewn onto women's clothing as a display of their wealth.

Above: American movie star Dorothy Lamour wears a spectacular sequinned evening gown which simply oozes Hollywood glamour, 1936.

Right: Bebe Daniels models a dress covered in silver sequins, which she wears with a headband featuring drop crystals, c.1920s.

Opposite: A portrait of Marie Antoinette by Louise Clay. Her hairdresser was one of her 'ministers of fashion'.

Right: An English fashion doll's mantua in silk, 1760s, used to demonstrate the maker's skill.

Decadent Dolls

Rose Bertin, the celebrated couturier, would call on her best customer, Marie Antoinette, Queen of France, twice a week. The two women would spend hours discussing fabric, texture, colour and cut. To try out new designs, they would dress dolls. These fashion dolls caught on and, until the advent of the mass-produced fashion magazine, became the standard calling card for a dressmaker.

Marie Antoinette's extravagance was breathtaking. It was not unusual for her to spend twenty times the annual wage of a skilled labourer – the equivalent of perhaps half a million dollars – on a single outfit. And the money was spent, her critics complained, on clothes that were at best inappropriate and at worst downright immoral. And she never wore an outfit a second time.

The *robe à la polonaise* was a style that swept Europe in the 1770s (see

page 32) – tight cut around the bodice, with front-fastening and skirts rustically hitched up at the sides in imitation of a milkmaid, exposing the ankles. In an age when noticing the queen's ankles was tantamount to treason, putting them on show was an act of shocking provocation. Even more shocking were her riding habits. Ladies were supposed to ride sidesaddle but Marie Antoinette straddled the horse like a man, and to do so had breeches – stylish breeches – specially made.

On 16 October 1793, the queen was sentenced to death by revolutionaries. On her way to the guillotine she wore a white chemise, with a large linen kerchief around her shoulders, and a white cap. She didn't wear this outfit a second time either.

Sumptuary Laws

To make sure the rich and powerful could shine in their fabulous clothes, at various times in history laws have been passed – usually called Sumptuary Laws – to make sure the poor and powerless looked appropriately dowdy.

In Imperial China there was a strict colour code for the various ranks of society. The poor were restricted to blue or black. Nero, Emperor of Rome, once had a woman dragged from the theatre and stripped naked in the public square for daring to wear the Imperial Purple.

Perhaps the most detailed of all the Sumptuary Laws were those enforced in old England. These specified, for instance, the top price a servant's wife should pay for a veil (12 pence) and the maximum length of the point on a commoner's shawl (5 cm/2 in). One centimetre (½ in) more meant jail.

Fancy Fabrics & *Deadly* Dyes

Until synthetic dyes were developed in the nineteenth century, using natural materials from plants and animals to dye fabric was a rather secret but safe art. Only royalty or the very rich could afford fabric dyed blue or purple but at least sea snail mucus, although smelly, wouldn't kill you.

Top: The murex shell was the source of the dye, Tyrian purple, used for imperial robes in ancient Rome.

Million Dollar Caterpillar

Legend has it that Leizu, Empress of China, was one day sitting in the sunshine, drinking tea. A cocoon, spun by a caterpillar, fell from a tree into her cup. The warmth of the tea made it unravel, revealing an extraordinary length of fine thread, which the empress had woven into a lustrous, lightweight fabric. Silk was born.

But it is no more than legend. Leizu lived in about 2700 BC. The earliest traces of silk fabric found in China date from 800 years before, at a time when Western Europeans had just started spinning wool, thrilling to the cutting-edge technology of the comb.

Silk farming, done the traditional way, is a brutal business. The caterpillars – silkworms – are carefully nurtured on

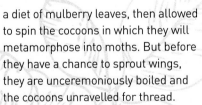

Left: A 1689 print shows Chinese women reeling silk, a delicate operation that required a light but consistent touch lest the silk break or become tangled.

Below: The American actress Carole Lombard in a bias-cut silk gown with kimono sleeves, 1932. The cut makes it cling to her body, almost like a second skin.

they liked. The breaking of the monopoly, in 552 AD, was one of the first and certainly one of the boldest feats of industrial espionage in history.

The superspies were two Persian monks. One day they turned up at the court of Justinian, Emperor of Byzantium, and announced that while visiting China on missionary work they had learnt the secrets of silk-making. In return for a huge sum of money, they agreed to return to China and bring back the means for the emperor

to start a domestic silk industry. Months later they returned, with silkworm eggs intrepidly smuggled in bamboo tubes, together with, presumably, a good supply of mulberry cuttings with which to feed the hatchlings.

In the West, silk remained a popular, although expensive, luxury until World War II, when shortages led to the use of alternatives. Out went silk stockings – for years a symbol of sex, glamour and luxury – and in came nylons. And the world grew a little less interesting.

a diet of mulberry leaves, then allowed to spin the cocoons in which they will metamorphose into moths. But before they have a chance to sprout wings, they are unceremoniously boiled and the cocoons unravelled for thread.

At times, the result was literally worth its weight in gold. The Roman senate tried several times to ban silk, not only on the grounds of cost, but also because, they suspected, its clinging, revealing nature was a threat to public morals.

Silks and Spies

For more than 4000 years the magic of the silkworm was a secret closely guarded by the Chinese silk farmers, whose monopoly allowed them to charge fashion fans in Asia, Africa and Europe pretty much whatever

Above: In this eighteenth-century colour lithograph a German dyer shows off his wares.

Right: A French gentleman of the late eighteenth century poses in a coat of 'Paris Green', which would have been impregnated with arsenic.

Classy Colours

Eighty thousand sea snails must be killed to make 1 ml (¹/₃ fl oz) of Tyrian purple dye. Due to the cost of such an operation, purple was traditionally the colour of kings and emperors. In Roman times, a child of such noble birth was said to be porphyrogenitos – born in the purple.

The colour comes from the snail's mucus, which meant not only were the nobles of ancient times dressed in snail snot, but they also stank. The smell of Tyrian purple never quite goes away. The city of Tyre, a great centre of production from which the colour takes its name, was an unbearably stinky place and the Roman nobility needed no fanfares to announce their arrival. You could smell them coming.

The cochineal, an insect native to South and Central America, is a little more productive than the Tyrian sea snail. Eighty thousand of them – whether boiled, baked or steamed – will yield nearly 500 g (1 lb) of the red dye that is still used as food colouring. Traditionally it put both the red in the 'Redcoats' of the British Army and the pink in the 'Pink' coats of stylish British foxhunters.

Colours to Die For

Some dyes require the deaths of plants or animals. Others kill people. Chrome yellow, when traditionally made, results in vomiting, cancer and death. Copper sulphate, used since ancient times as a 'mordant' to 'stick' many different pigments to fabric, can corrode the skin and eyes, and rot the liver.

Estaesfigura deun nopal estadetodopunto cultibado ylacochi nilla aensambrado bien yansiestanlos yndios Gocando desucOsecha

Left: Spanish dyers harvest the cochineal insect from a stand of prickly pear, 1620.

Below: An English officer of the 13th Light Dragoons in uniform, his 'redcoat' dyed with cochineal, 1831.

One of the most notorious of all dyestuffs was Scheele's Green, developed by the chemist Carl Wilhelm Scheele in the late eighteenth century and used in fashion and interior décor to brilliant, although often fatal, effect. The problem was arsenic, a crucial ingredient and a deadly poison. A later variant, known as 'Paris Green', was indeed so toxic that it was sold as rat poison as well as a dyestuff. It is thought that Napoleon Bonaparte, one of the greatest generals of all time, was finally slain not by his enemies but by the green wallpaper in his bedroom, which, it is suspected, gave off arsenical fumes. Green sweets are widely treated with suspicion – a folk memory of the days when Paris Green was used, inconceivably, as a food colouring.

In the mid-nineteenth century, when the truth about the colour's toxicity was finally realised, the shock was severe. As the *London Times* put it: 'What manufactured article in these days of high pressure civilisation can possibly be trusted if socks are dangerous?'.

Accessorise
or Die

There was a time when a woman just wouldn't be seen in public without her hat and gloves. Nowadays she has pared down her accessories so much that she needs a huge handbag, called a tote, to carry all her other essentials. It may not contain a snuffbox or a lorgnette, but among the detritus at the bottom of her bag there may lurk a pair of sunglasses or a collapsible umbrella.

Head on a Plate

The ruff first appeared in the early sixteenth century as a modest lace collar gathered by a drawstring around the neck, but it quickly developed into an elaborate construction in which a wired frame was covered with fluted starched linen, often embroidered with gold and silver needlework and edged with lace. This gleaming white circle, which framed the head, separating it from the body, rather like a platter, was designed to protect the wearer's clothing and be easier to replace than a soiled dress or shirt.

It had no practical value. Not only was it uncomfortable to wear, a great bother to look after and wilted when wet, but also a top-quality one cost a fortune – in other words it was the perfect show-off accessory. Fashionable in Western Europe in the second half of the sixteenth century, it came and went in about fifty years.

At the height of the fashion, the rich wore ruffs made of up to 5–6 m (5–6 yd) of fine fabric, often trimmed with lace, fashioned into hundreds of intricate pleats. The best would be gossamer fine and sparkle with jewels resembling not so much a garment as an aura.

The 'setting' of a ruff required the services of a professional launderer who used liberal amounts of starch and wire supports called 'suppertasses' to construct their little sculptures. The pleats were formed around shaped metal rods, often heated in a fire.

The most extreme version was the 'cartwheel' ruff, which was up to 6 or 8 cm (2½ or 3 in) deep, big enough to extend well beyond the shoulders. Henry III of France wore a ruff made from an extraordinary 16 m (17 yd) of fabric, while one French lady was so

…one French lady was so inconvenienced by her ruff that she had to use a spoon with a 50-cm (1½ ft) handle to eat her soup.

inconvenienced by hers that she had to use a spoon with a 50-cm (1½-ft) handle to eat her soup.

Attacked by English Puritans such as Phillip Stubbes, who called them 'cartwheels of the devil's chariot of pride', ruffs had vanished by the middle of the seventeenth century, making only a faltering return visit in the nineteenth in the shape of uncomfortably tall, stiff collars. 'He looks in that deep ruff,' said the English dramatist and poet Ben Jonson, 'like a head on a platter.'

The fashion died out as quickly as it had appeared. These days ruffs are seen only on choirboys and circus dogs.

Starch

With its fine lace-makers, Flanders was one of the early centres for starch-making, and it was the Dutch who introduced starch to the Elizabethan court. Made from boiling bran or other grains in water, it was ladled over both sides of the ruff in an attempt to keep it stiff even in wet weather. Some enterprising manufacturers tried to promote coloured starch but it was regarded as decadent. Blue starch, which made ruffs and collars look whiter than white, remained the popular choice.

Stick It!

A stick, any sort of stick, invites swagger. As an object of high fashion, it came into its own in Europe around the time that gentlemen abandoned the sword as acceptable daywear. Women, who wanted to swagger too, took it up as a shepherdessy adjunct to the polonaise look of the 1770s. The sticks of this period were worn long, sometimes up to the shoulder, and were a boon when it came to balancing on the ultra-high heels that were also in vogue at the time.

By the end of the nineteenth century a reputable cane shop would have had in stock a dozen or so types of cane, each with its own property and name – the supplejack, the whangee, the kebbie, the Penang Lawyer.

As well as providing flounce and figure, the stick became an ideal medium for showing off wealth. Fabergé made sticks exquisitely decorated with gold, black nephrite and enamel for the Russian royal family. Tiffany made dress-sticks with tops of intricately carved solid silver. There were sticks encrusted with diamonds, inlaid with jade and ivory, sticks made of perfumed wood.

And there were dual-function sticks, which doubled as a place to hide a jigger or two of whisky, a sword, a gun, a camera or even, in one case, a tiny but tuneful trumpet.

Posh Parasols and Upmarket Umbrellas

In a bas-relief sculpture from the ancient Kingdom of Nineveh, dating from the eighth century BC, an important personage, probably a king, rides in a chariot. To protect the king's bald head from the sun, a servant holds a parasol.

Both the parasol, which protects us from the sun, and its cousin the umbrella, which protects us from the rain, have been with us a long time. In the Egypt of the pharaohs, elaborate and ornamental parasols were constructed from palm leaves and coloured feathers. In Tibetan Buddhism, the Umbrella – along with the Endless Knot, the Fish and the Wheel – is one of the Eight Auspicious Symbols. Beneath its canopy, all can take refuge.

The tiered umbrella, seen in China, Siam and many neighbouring countries, was a possibly pointless elaboration on the basic theme, with several canopies arranged one above the other on the same stick. Usually the number of tiers indicated the status of the user. One Burmese King was described as 'Lord of The Twenty Four Sunshades'.

The great technological breakthrough in umbrella design came in the first century AD when a Chinese genius (his or her name is lost to history), invented the collapsible parasol, essentially identical to the modern version – ribs were attached to a short tube that can run up and down the shaft.

Evidence of umbrella use in medieval Europe is sparse, and the collapsible model was unknown. The first inklings of its wonders came in the seventeenth century, when Catholic missionaries to

China brought examples home as souvenirs. The French and Italians readily adopted it for sun and for rain – the ladies' sunshades, like their walking sticks, being built primarily for swagger and featuring a tiny, token canopy on the end of a good, flounceable length of stick. Only later did these evolve into something more practical, prettified with floral patterns, lace and fringing.

But in England, although fashionable ladies took to the parasol, for men the umbrella was regarded as a Frenchified frivolity. Englishmen, it was thought, could take a wetting. The man who broke the mould was Jonas Hanway, an intrepid traveller and philanthropist who, in about 1750, began to carry an umbrella in the streets of London. He was mocked. He was accused of being French. But he persisted and, over time, where he led others followed. By the early 1900s the English had embraced the umbrella to the extent that a black one, tightly rolled, along with the bowler hat, had become an essential part of the businessman's uniform.

Traditional Japanese Umbrellas

Earlier versions of the Japanese umbrella were used to protect the emperor and nobility from the sun and evil spirits, but until the invention of the modern collapsible umbrella peasants had to make do with straw hats and capes. The delicate, beautiful *wagasa*, a traditional umbrella, is hand-made from natural materials – using tapioca glue, *washi* paper is fixed to a frame of up to 70 bamboo ribs. A single umbrella may take four craftsmen 2 months to make.

Left: In this 1788 fashion print, a fashionista wears a polonaise and protects her pale complexion with a fringed parasol that is smaller than her hairdo.

Right: Traditional Japanese *wagasa* or umbrellas are still made with *washi* paper, hand-made from bark fibres.

...for men the umbrella was regarded as a Frenchified frivolity. Englishmen, it was thought, could take a wetting.

emotions – disgust, delight, dismay, disbelief. And best of all was the snuffbox, which could be tiny, tasteful and expensive enough to both electrify and astound.

The only feature common to all snuffboxes is an airtight lid; damp snuff is hard to sniff. Otherwise they have been made from every material imaginable, from wood and papier-mâché to silver and gold, inlaid with enamel, adorned with precious stones, carved from a single agate – there is no end to the possibilities. Some, like lockets, contained a picture of a loved one, while others were fashioned into rather curious shapes – fruits, flowers, animals, shoes, even skulls. Ceramic boxes were often painted with portraits, landscapes, historical and biblical scenes, providing the miniaturist with a perfect canvas for showing off his skill.

The dandy would have a different snuffbox for every day of the year. 'It is by this touch of distinction,' said one Parisian commentator in 1781, 'that we may recognise the man of taste'.

The Cigarette Holder

Another useful accessory for those with a predeliction for elegant affectation was the cigarette holder, popular with women in particular from about 1910 to the 1970s. Typically made from bakelite, silver or jade, it included a filter and prevented the smoker from developing nicotine-stained fingers.

Giant Pockets and Ridicules

When women's clothes were multi-layered and voluminous, pockets, sometimes called 'bagges', could be made huge and secreted within the folds of the skirt, with a slit cut for access. One old lady was reported

A nineteenth-century wooden snuffbox, with inlay, in the form of a boot.

Nose in the Air

The late eighteenth century should be called the Age of Accessorisation. It was an age when progressive fops, inspired by a spirit of fearless investigation, sought out new props to prettify, exploring every avenue of posing potential.

In refined circles at this time, tobacco smoking was out. Gentlemen of quality – and some ladies – took snuff instead. The ritual of snuff-taking – snorting powdered tobacco up the nose – was a gift for the *poseur*. The delicate pinch, the sniff, the sneeze, the handkerchief could all be choreographed variously to express a whole lexicon of moods and

As the century progressed, ridicules grew bigger and more elaborate. Usually handmade, they demonstrated a woman's skill with embroidery, crocheting or ribbon-work. The modern clutch, the tote and the bucket are all descendents of these Victorian constructions, and although the smelling-bottle and nutmeg-grater are rarely found among their contents, the biscuit crumbs are probably a permanent fixture.

Left: In its heyday, the 1920s, a woman's cigarette holder could be of different lengths – opera, theatre, dinner or cocktail, according to the social occasion.

Below: An embroidered red velvet pocket, from Germany, 1775–1825.

to have in one pocket a handkerchief and coins, and in another, 'a pocket-book, a bunch of keys, a needle case, a spectacle-case, crumbs of biscuit, a nutmeg and grater, a smelling-bottle and an apple'.

In the early nineteenth century, the layered look gave way to the Empire line dress, a much simpler gown of flimsy fabric, cut tight at the bodice, with nowhere to hide so much as a hankie. Accordingly, 'pockets' evolved into dainty drawstring handbags, made of silk or satin and often embroidered. They came to be called 'indispensables' or 'reticules', which quickly became corrupted to 'ridicules'.

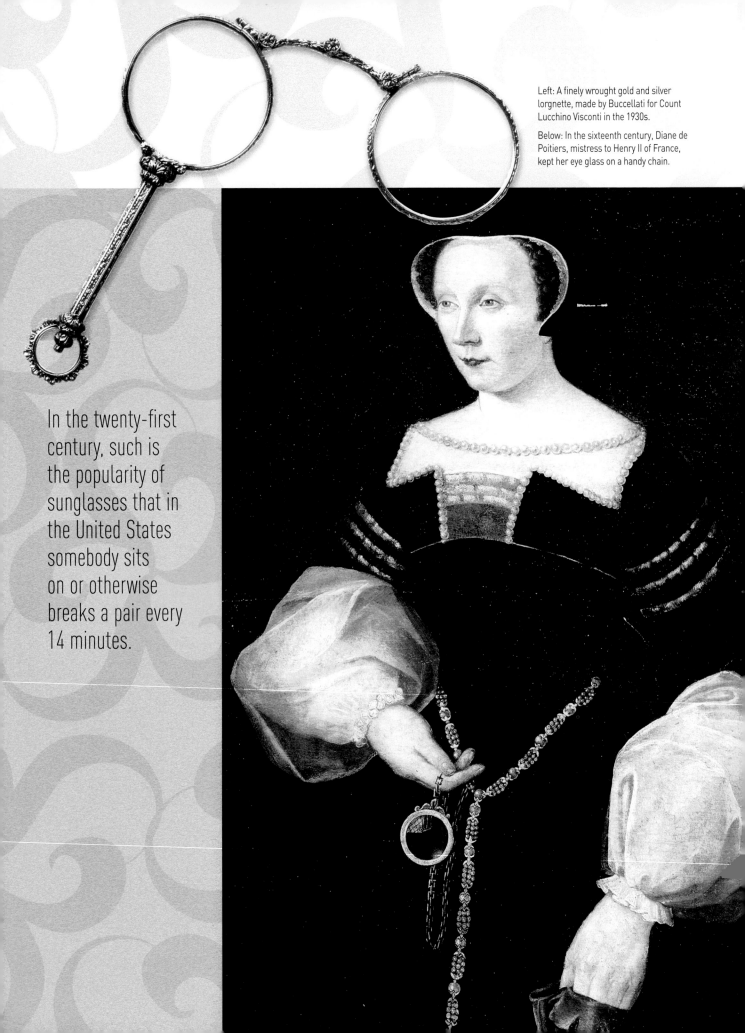

In the twenty-first century, such is the popularity of sunglasses that in the United States somebody sits on or otherwise breaks a pair every 14 minutes.

Specs Appeal

Until the brave pioneers of the Age of Accessorisation seized on them, spectacles – although they'd been around since the thirteenth century – had languished in the ugly drawer, their use restricted to scholars and geeks.

The first designer specs – or spec – was the Quizzing Glass, a single lens on a stick. In the hands of a fop or a lady of fashion it could be used to devastating effect. Confronted with a new person or *objet,* the quizzer, with a great flourish, would produce the glass – intricately and expensively wrought, of course, from precious metals and inset with gemstones. The item in question would be flamboyantly scrutinised, then judgment would be passed. The activity acquired its own dictionary definition: Quizzing – the act of mocking by close examination.

In 1770, optician George Adams invented a two-lensed version of the Quizzing Glass that became known as a lorgnette. Although it never quite achieved the fashionable cachet of the Quizzing Glass, the lorgnette was still being used by disapproving aunts and headmistresses to criticise and terrify well into the twentieth century.

Ingenious Victorians devised versions in which one lens folded over the other and retracted into the handle to form a compact package that could be hung from a chain. There was even a spring-loaded lorgnette which, at the press of a button, would explode from its handle like a switchblade.

Towards the end of the nineteenth century, gents with defective vision who shunned the bookishness of spectacles would often sport a monocle, a single lens jammed into the eye socket. But it was always a precarious compromise. A raised eyebrow at luncheon could all too easily propel it into the soup.

During World War I, the monocle's popularity with German generals caused it to fall out of favour in the United Kingdom.

Dark Glasses

Dark glasses have been protecting eyes from the sun since at least the twelfth century, but the need for designer shades wasn't felt until the twentieth century. In the 1920s, first the French then the rest of the Caucasian world decided a tan looked good, and opticians were quick to exploit the new market. Early sunglasses tended to look like medical supplies, but in 1936 a pair of lightweight glasses with advanced filtering characteristics was developed for pilots. The result, Ray-Ban Aviators – arguably the first-ever cool sunglasses – became pretty much standard wear for the US military in World War II. In the twenty-first century, such is the popularity of sunglasses that in the United States somebody sits on or otherwise breaks a pair every 14 minutes. The most expensive sunglasses currently on the market cost a third of a million US dollars. Their only exceptional feature is the designer's logo, which is inlaid with diamonds.

Right: These butterfly sunglasses would not be out of place at a masked ball.

Left: An Art Nouveau design for a fan by Alphonse Mucha, 1899.

Below: The invention of the folding fan is said to have been inspired by a bat's wing. An ingenious innovation, it provided a wider area for decoration and more scope for elegant wrist action.

Fan Clubs

Tutankhamun was buried with eight fans – seven big ones and a small one. It was thought that fans could 'restore the breath of life to the deceased'.

Hand-held fans became popular in Europe in about the fourteenth century. Portraits of Elizabeth I of England often show her holding a fan, usually in the shape of a ping-pong bat, although towards the end of her reign the queen, along with the rest of Europe, took to using that exciting technological innovation from the East, the folding fan. As the sixteenth century evolved into the seventeenth, the sound of people fiddling with these irritating little gizmos began to infuriate. At the court of Louis XIV of France, etiquette demanded they remained firmly closed in the presence of the king or queen.

Early models were usually painted with allegorical or pastoral scenes but tastes soon ran to novelty. There were fans printed with rules for card games or witty riddles, even fortune-telling fans. It's a myth that fans were used to convey secret messages to suitors but they were undoubtedly used to convey a lady's mood – the angry snap, the timorous quiver, the amorous flutter.

Japanese Fans

The first fans appeared in Japan in about the sixth century. Stiff and flat, like large leaves, they comprised a circular frame made from a bamboo stick, sliced and splayed and covered with silk or *washi* paper, hand-made from bark fibres. Decorated with suns, moons, sacred texts or mini-landscapes, fans were used by actors and dancers during performances, by generals on the battlefield signalling to their troops and sometimes by folk just trying to keep cool in the stifling summer heat.

About the close of the nineteenth century the fan had reached some sort of limit in size and popularity as ostrich feather fans reaching 46 cm (18 in) across coincided with a fashion for leg-of-mutton sleeves. Then two world wars expunged such frippery from women's lives as they found that, on evenings out, they needed both hands free for drinking and smoking.

Above: An Art Nouveau illustration by the French artist Georges Barbier, c.1925.

Right: A Japanese woman poses with her *uchiwa*, a simple flat model used for fanning the face, 1900.

Left: In this 1843 portrait by Joseph-Désiré Court, a woman is dressed for a masked ball in a pink satin cloak and white gloves.

Below: According to a traditional French method for citing glove lengths, this glove, suitable for day wear, is 'six buttons' long.

Glove Love

Warm hands have always been desirable, and when you're walking through thorns or napping flints in the Stone Age, some sort of protection is prudent, too.

Tomb raiders have found gloves buried with the pharaohs, including one exquisite pair, sewn from linen, decorated with a leaf pattern and with laces to tie them to the wrists or perhaps to the coat, like an infant's.

But despite their antiquity, gloves didn't catch on as a fashion accessory until the thirteenth century, when gentlewomen wore them long, and finely stitched from silk or linen. The vanity of such luxuries shocked decent people. Nuns were forbidden to wear them, and laws banning them were passed in Bologna, Rome and most other upright places.

Although silk and linen had their attractions, the finest gloves were leather, which could be made to fit like a second skin and soaked in perfume that would linger forever. The thinner the leather, the better the glove. In the seventeenth century they made them from chicken skin. 'Limerick' gloves were made from the skin of unborn calves.

Peeling off a fine leather glove was: 1) a useful ploy when you needed time to think; 2) a great way of drawing attention to your beautiful white hand; and 3) disconcertingly erotic.

Napoleon Bonaparte was something of a glove fetishist. He had a personal collection of 240 pairs and foisted them on his Josephine and other women of the court.

But the glove's golden age is the middle of the nineteenth century when the *mousquetaire*, also known as an 'Opera Glove' or an 'Evening Glove', came to stay. In kidskin, with three buttons at the wrist and three lines embroidered on the back of the hand, it reached to just above the elbow. They were worn tight. Too tight. Dousing your arms in cold water and powdering them helped, but it could still take a long time to lever in chubby wrists.

By the twentieth century, gloves – long for evening, short for day – were mandatory. In 1961, a book of etiquette, published in New York, stressed most vehemently that no woman should ever appear in public without gloves, and she should take them off only for eating, smoking or playing cards, never for dancing or shaking hands, although she may remove one glove when canapés are passed round.

Above: Possibly made in England by the Sheldon Tapestry Workshops in the sixteenth or seventeenth century, this extraordinary white leather gauntlet features tapestry woven with silk and gold.

Right: Reminiscent of an amphibian costume for a 1950s horror movie, these green and gold leather gloves are by the Italian fashion designer, Elsa Schiaparelli, 1939. Only the claws are missing.

Baubles, Bangles & Beads

Few would argue that a bakelite bangle is more attractive than a diamond bracelet, yet even jewellery made of dried pasta has had its moment in the spotlight. Sometimes it's simply a matter of what you have to hand. The Aztecs had lots of gold, and De Beers had diamonds, but the Punks only had packets of safety pins.

Top: The gold Scarab Pectoral, found in Tutankhamun's tomb, is inlaid with lapis lazuli, red carnelian and turquoise.

The Wandering Pearl

With their unique lustre and subtle illuminating effect on a woman's skin, pearls – a curious accident of oyster biology – have at times been valued more highly than diamonds, rubies or gold. And prized above all pearls is La Peregrina – the wanderer.

Originally weighing 223.8 grains (about 56 carats), La Peregrina is not the biggest pearl ever found, nor is it the most perfect, but it features the best story. An African slave discovered it in 1513 near the Pearl Islands off the Pacific coast of Panama. He handed it over to his Spanish masters and in return, so legend says, he was given his freedom.

In turn the Spaniards presented it to their king and in 1554, Prince Philip of Spain gave La Peregrina to Mary I of England, as an engagement present.

Above: The Cartier necklace owned by Elizabeth Taylor, featuring the La Peregrina pearl.

Above right: French singer Gaby Deslys (1881–1920) with her string of pearls valued at half a million dollars.

Left: Queen Mary I of England, 1554, shown wearing a necklace featuring the La Peregrina pearl.

After Mary's death, it was returned to the Spanish royal family.

In 1808, Napoleon Bonaparte conquered Spain and installed his brother Joseph as king. When Joseph, deposed, fled back to France, he took the pearl with him. He bequeathed it to his nephew Charles Louis – the man who, until his disastrous dethronement in 1870, ruled France as Napoleon III. Broke and living as an exile in London, this Napoleon sold the pearl to the Marquess of Abercorn, whose wife promptly lost it, twice – both times in appropriately regal surroundings: at Buckingham Palace it fell from its setting and hitched a ride on the train of another courtier's dress, and at Windsor Castle it vanished down the back of a sofa.

It remained in the insecure hands of the Dukes of Abercorn until 1969, when movie star Richard Burton bought it as a Valentine's present for his wife, Elizabeth Taylor. She, too, lost it, again in a palace – Caesar's Palace hotel in Las Vegas. After conducting a tuft by tuft search of the shag pile carpet in her room, she eventually realised that the bone her Pekingese puppy was chewing was not a bone after all.

After Taylor's death, La Peregrina was sold to a 'private Asian buyer' for US$11.8 million.

The undisputed 'kings of bling' were
the Aztecs of Central America.

Left: What an Aztec king
might have worn in the
seventeenth century.

Below: This gold
necklace would have
been worn by the Mixtec
people in present-day
Mexico, c.1300–1521.

Ancient Bling

As well as food, air and the usual
requirements of life there seems to be
a fundamental human need to shine.
Luckily gold, most people's bling of
choice for 5000 years or more, stays
shiny forever.

Well-heeled Mesopotamians sported
necklaces crafted from gold and set
with agate and lapis lazuli. The people of
the Indus Valley fashioned gold chokers,
rings and bangles of extraordinary
beauty and delicacy, inset with rubies
sapphires and emeralds. Tutankhamun,
the Egyptian pharaoh, was buried with
a billion dollars worth of the stuff.

But the undisputed 'kings of bling'
were the Aztecs of Central America. So
productive were their mines that their
attitude to gold was slightly different to
that found in the rest of the world. They
called it *teocuitlati* – 'the excrement of
the gods' – and used it with unsparing
abandon. They filed down their teeth
and inlaid them with gold. They wore
gold pins in their noses and plugs in

Right: An artificial silk dress with Art Deco patterning, 1927.

Below: A gold Egyptian snake ring , from the first century AD.

Bottom: Perfect for the bling fan who likes to get their point across – a diamond-encrusted ring in the shape of a dollar sign.

their ears. They even fashioned gold nose covers to make their profiles conform to the arrow-straight-from-brow-to-tip aristocratic profile to which all Aztecs aspired. Women used gold straps as a form of brassiere to lift and separate. Warriors used gold in their armour. Priests wore gold masks. The Spanish Conquistadors who destroyed the Aztecs claimed to fight for God, Glory and Gold, although most of them would have settled for one out of three.

Modern Bling

Can you see my jewellery from a mile away? Nothing says rich like a wall of diamonds. Hip Hop grew out of the backstreets of the Bronx in the 1970s and brought us rap, graffiti, deejaying, breakdancing and bling, or bling-bling. The name is the sound that light makes when it bounces off something so shiny it's a blindness hazard. Bling, done properly, should be costly and really, really big. Chains should be mayoral, rings should immobilise the hand,

buckles should be the size of corsets. Platinum and gold are the only acceptable materials and, wherever possible, they should be icy with diamonds. The vajazzle – an application of bling to what may euphemistically be called the bikini area – has been adopted widely; the pezazzle, a male version of the same thing, less so.

Dress Like an Egyptian

When Howard Carter and George Herbert discovered Tutankhamun's tomb of treasures in 1922, they unleashed 'Tutmania', a craze that influenced fashion trends for the next twenty years as well as the geometric shapes and sunbursts of Art Deco. 'Flappers' of the 1920s wore serpent-like gold cuff bracelets studded with gems such as rhinestones set close together, layers of necklaces and headbands like those worn by the pharaoh himself.

De Beers

Invention of the Engagement Ring

Diamonds are not the rarest of gemstones but their unique sparkle guarantees them a price above rubies, which coincidentally *are* the rarest. The Victorians fell in love with their brilliant sparkle, which was intensified by the blue flicker of gaslight. But between the world wars of the twentieth century, diamond sales slumped. De Beers, the world's biggest diamond producer, fought back with the biggest advertising campaign ever launched.

At this time the ring was merely one among many possible tokens that a man might give his intended upon their engagement. In some European countries, even a cheap thimble was considered acceptable.

De Beers decided to promote the notion that it had to be a ring – and more particularly a diamond ring – with a worldwide advertising campaign and slogan, the so-called 'four words that changed industry' – 'A diamond is forever'.

Sales soared. Diamonds became a girl's best friend, and their status as the only symbols of true love worth trusting was firmly planted in the human psyche.

The De Beers slogan – eventually translated into twenty-nine languages and voted 'Best Advertising Slogan of the Twentieth Century' – was originally coined by Frances Gerety, a copywriter at the New York agency, N. W. Ayer & Son. She never married.

From Plastic to Safety Pins

In fashionable Victorian society nobody would dare to wear 'paste' jewellery. Better no jewels at all than to be accused of fraud. But in the early part of the twentieth century, the Art Deco movement, which put more emphasis on shape and 'the look' than on intrinsic worth, along with the development of new metallic alloys, plastics and bakelite, resulted in a change of attitude. 'Costume' jewellery could be judged in its own right as cheap but nonetheless stylish fun. The phrase 'done up like a Christmas tree' was no longer an indictment.

With World War II came a necessary fashion for home-made jewellery. Metal was for manufacturing aeroplanes and battleships. The women's magazines cheerfully encouraged patriotic creativity and featured instructions for making brooches from dried spaghetti, earrings from seashells and corsages from wax-dipped cloth.

In a perverse way, this wartime spirit was revived in the 1970s. The Punk movement embraced do-it-yourself.

Safety pins were used as piercings, toilet chains were pressed into service as necklaces, a razor blade became a pendant, padlocks replaced buttons. Although the press warned that Punk would bring about the end of civilisation as we know it, most parents prayed that nothing would go septic.

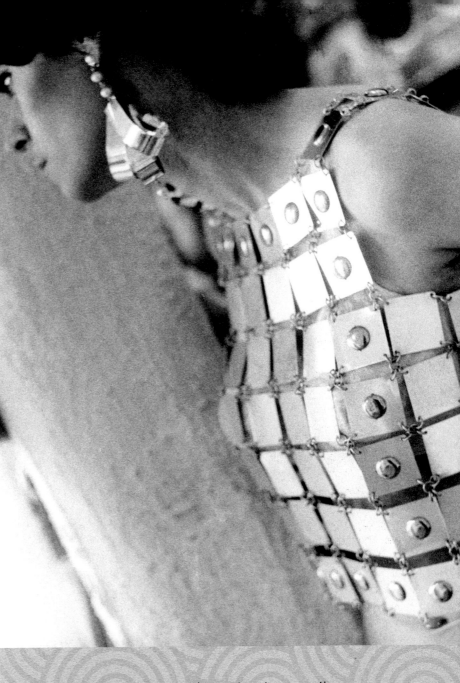

Safety pins were used as piercings, toilet chains were pressed into service as necklaces, a razor blade became a pendant, padlocks replaced buttons.

Top: A young Swedish Punk has punctured his face with safety pins, 1977.

Above: The model's enamel drop earrings are teamed with a white plastic bangle, 1962.

Above: Paco Rabanne designed this dress of linked plastic squares in 1967. Around this time designers were experimenting with new materials.

Fur & Feathers

The birds of the air and beasts of the field have over the years proved themselves invaluable, dead or alive, as fashion accessories. From ancient Romans with dogs up their sleeves, to freaks with firefly hair, from royal personages swathed in moles, to disco divas with goldfish in their shoes, the relationship between fur, feathers and fashion has been quirky, controversial and nearly always fatal.

Right: A woman tries on capes made from hare and rabbit in a furrier's shop, c.1845.

Why Wear Fur?

The first clothes ever worn were skins and furs, but it was never just about warmth – the idea that an animal hide magically imbues the wearer with the animal qualities is both ancient and deep-rooted.

By the Middle Ages the aristocracy were wearing furs as a luxurious trim on tunics, cloaks and hats; men utilised fur's superior insulation by wearing fur coats with the fur inside.

Fur and fur-trimmed dresses, coats and hats were all the rage in Victorian times. Even top hats could be made of beaver fur, a North American import of great economic importance at the time.

In the 1920s, when flappers were shortening their skirts and everyone was letting their inner animal off the leash, male American college students fell prey to an unstoppable craze for full-length raccoon-skin coats. Even though the raccoon is known for neither its courage nor its ferocity, the coats were supposed to indicate that every physics nerd and Keats enthusiast was, at heart, a frontiersman.

Similarly a woman dressed in, or decorously arranged on, for instance, a leopard skin – even a fake leopard skin – might have been suggesting she was a wild cat possessed of dangerous animal passions.

Minks and Martens

In summer, the fur of the stoat is thin, rough and dull brown, but its winter coat is silky, dense and – in the best examples – pure white with contrasting black flecks. This winter coat, known as ermine, is used to line the crowns of kings, decorate their coats-of-arms and carpet their pavilions. Like ermine, the fur of a sable, a species of marten prized for its softness and lustre, has traditionally been a gift fit for a king. By 1952 it was generally accepted, in the United States at least, that the woman who didn't want mink was socially defective. Those who couldn't afford a full-length coat would comfort themselves with a stole, or even a tiny mink brooch, to tide themselves over until their luck changed.

The fur coat

Until 1850, although fur was used extensively for trimmings and accessories, only Inuit people and others who frequented the frozen North or South wore a fur coat. The fashion for fur coats may have been triggered by a display of coats, made from various furs, shown at the London Great Exhibition of 1851. Certainly when the motorcar came along – the early models were inevitably open-topped – something warm and cuddly was an essential accessory.

In these early years, beaver fur, used as a felt by the hat industry for generations, was the most popular, along with sealskin and fox. Queen

Above: It is difficult to appreciate the appeal of a fur stole that requires the services of a taxidermist.

Right: In the 1960s a mink coat was a fashion prize coveted by many but afforded only by a few.

Alexandra, the wife of Edward VII of the United Kingdom, wore a coat made of moleskin, hoping to set a fashion that would help rid Scottish farmers of a terrible pest. It didn't catch on.

Hollywood made the fur coat a must-have. Right back to the silent era, even in the heat of the California summer, movie stars liked to be photographed wearing their fur coats.

Taking a walk with a
wild animal on a leash –
specially flown in from
Kenya, of course – is
an inspired but possibly
perilous alternative to
wearing furs.

Above: A leopard fur coat with a shawl collar, 1963.

Opposite: While shopping in London in 1939, American
silent film actress Phyllis Gordon, her shoulders
draped in a full fox stole, takes her cheetah for a stroll.

Frothy Feathers

For humans, as for birds, feathers are made for flaunting, although in ancient times they would have been worn for warmth as well. In many cultures, both ancient and modern, feathers have had cultural and religious significance.

In imitation of their gods, Aztec nobility clothed themselves in feathered headdresses and wore great cloaks of feathers – the brighter and bigger the plumage, the more important the wearer. Hawaiian royalty wore capes of mesh into which bright feathers were woven in patterns of red, yellow and black. Chiefs and their wives wore ropes of feathers as garlands or leis around their heads and necks.

In contrast, Europeans and urban Americans always seemed to have had their doubts about feathered frocks. Although the nineteenth-century enthusiasm for feathered hats was apparently insatiable, inexplicably plumage was seldom seen below the neck.

The Columbine, a traditional half-mask worn during Venice's Carnevale, is decorated with feathers, gold and silver. Feather boas of maribou, ostrich or turkey have come and gone since the seventeenth century, but they are still strongly associated with 1920s flappers and 'exotic dancers'. And for a decade or so, in Jane Austen's day, the Regency fashions featured swan's down tippets – long, slender scarves like boas – and feather muffs for keeping hands warm.

Above left: An off-the-shoulder gown teamed with a cloche hat, both adorned with feathers, 1920.

Left: In an illustrated advertisement for Hair by Émile, the fan of feathers somehow complements the bird's nest hairdo.

Although the nineteenth-century enthusiasm for feathered hats was apparently insatiable, inexplicably plumage was seldom seen below the neck.

Protest

The feather trade was the first to provoke protest. In the United Kingdom, alarm at the number of birds being slaughtered, principally for hats, led in 1869 to the passing of the Sea Birds Preservation Act – the world's first conservation law – and the foundation of the Royal Society for the Protection of Birds. The Audubon Society in the United States, the Gould League in Australia and similar societies in other parts of the world also raised the voice of protest, which led to the widespread outlawing of the trade. Meanwhile Queen Alexandra led the fashion for bird-friendlier hats by banning the wearing of osprey feathers at court – a small measure, but nonetheless significant. (See also page 120.)

Above left: A white evening dress with ostrich feathers by the Spanish couturier Balenciaga, 1967.

Left: Detail of a feathered evening dress in silk, cotton and organza by Christian Dior, 1967.

During the 1930s, there was a short-lived fashion for the feathered capelet, a sleeveless jacket usually decorated with ostrich feathers. Its decline was partly due to the sneezing fits provoked by stray feathers.

Live Accessories

There is nothing new about the handbag dog. The aristocratic ladies of ancient Rome could often be seen with a *Canis Melitaeus*, a Maltese, peeping from a sleeve. Similarly, one of the oldest breeds of dog, the Pekingese, could be found up the sleeve of a Chinese emperor. Elizabeth I of England was known to clutch a small spaniel, and sometimes even wore a monkey on her shoulder. The function of these animals was always more than decorative – they were useful as feet warmers on cold nights or on cold journeys, and were also supposed to act as magnets for their owner's fleas.

4
millinery madness

If a woman rebels against high-heeled shoes, she should take care to do it in a very smart hat.

GEORGE BERNARD SHAW, 1856–1950

Headdresses

Ancient cultures adopted headdresses that delivered a clear message about the wearer's status, while in medieval times European women would have been roundly chastised if they had stepped out of the door without covering their heads. The desire to make these 'coverings' decorative soon occupied the female imagination, and they were transformed over the centuries into bold, beautiful and often almost entirely impractical fashion statements.

Above: On the solid gold burial mask of Tutankhamun (c.1370–1352 BC), the *nemes* is striped with gold and blue glass.

Predatory Egyptian Headdresses

The *nemes*, the headdress of the ancient Egyptian pharaohs – a single striped piece of cloth, bound tightly across the forehead with two loose pieces hanging down on either side, the back gathered into a plait – was to become one of the most distinctive features of their costume and helped to convey a truly regal hauteur. The Egyptian nobility wore a simpler version called the *khat*, which sported neither stripes nor pleats.

From the forehead part of the headdress, the golden head of Wadjet, the cobra goddess, or Nekhbet, the vulture goddess, rose up in predatory fashion. This style of headdress, seen in the famous death mask of the pharoah Tutankhamun, is carved on the heads of the enigmatic sphinxes brooding in splendid isolation over their desert kingdom.

Right: A French woman wears a ram's horn headdress with a fur-trimmed brocade jacket over a woollen dress, c.1420.

With its ethereal veil, the steeple headdress was to become the preferred headgear of fairy tale princesses through the ages.

Horned Headdresses

The huge sculpted curves of the ram's horn headdress, popular in Europe in the mid-fifteenth century, made it one of the most extraordinary styles of the age. Two large horns, sometimes 1 m (3 ft) in length and made out of mesh or leather secured to a skullcap, protruded rather ferociously from a woman's temples. Gauze veils hanging from each end softened the horns, but the modest and retiring effect was deftly subverted on ceremonial occasions, when the horns were trimmed with a triumphant display of ornaments and flags.

Steeple Headdresses

A desire to achieve height rather than width was to find expression in the hennin or 'steeple' headdress of the fifteenth century, which rose somewhat precariously from the head in a tall, thin cone covered with silk or velvet. A gauze veil attached to its point floated down romantically to the shoulders, and the whole construction was firmly anchored by a close-fitting undercap with sturdy ties. Essentially a continental style, it originated in Burgundy; the word *hennin* comes from the Old French *genhennen*, meaning 'inconvenience'.

It certainly lived up to its name when it towered a dizzying metre (3 ft) or more into the air, imitating the soaring Gothic spires of the time and appearing to express the wearer's desire, through her headwear at least, to move closer to the heavens. With its ethereal veil, the steeple headdress was to become the preferred headgear of fairy tale princesses through the ages.

Right: The hennin or steeple headdress featured a flimsy veil that could come forward to hide the wearer's face or float elegantly down the back.

Above: A young woman models a butterfly head-dress with a wimple attachment, 1435.

Eventually, ram's horns and 'henins' were replaced by the even more spectacular butterfly headdress, which was popular in Europe until the late fifteenth century.

Tubular Headdresses

The ancient Cangyuan rock paintings of China's Yunnan Province depict people wearing tall headdresses made of such animal materials as ox horns and antlers, feathers and tiger tails. Today Chinese minorities still wear often elaborate headdresses – made from plants, animals and minerals sourced locally – that reflect their age, marital status and religious beliefs, or to symbolise qualities such as courage and strength.

The red silk *boghtaq*, originally a Mongol headdress, was a tall hollow cylinder surmounting a cap with wings and topped with a gilded, silk-covered board decorated with silver wire. When the Venetian explorer Marco Polo souvenired one on his travels through China during the thirteenth century, the *boghtaq* was conventional wear for married Chinese women of the aristocracy. Perhaps it was the inspiration for the steeple headdress that became the fashion in Europe a few hundred years later.

Butterfly Headdress

Eventually, ram's horns and hennins were replaced by the even more spectacular butterfly headdress, which was popular in Europe until the late fifteenth century. This rather complex confection, which rose high above the head, was made out of wire and attached to a small cap that enclosed the hair. A diaphanous veil floated out from its twin points in the shape of a butterfly's wings. Worn by hard-working matrons as well as the high-born, it found favour with religious orders who adopted its fly-away veil – unlike the hennin and the ram's horn headdress, both denounced as evil by clerics.

Modern Headdresses

In the 1920s, milliners drew inspiration from both history and other cultures. The flapper's headband, adorned with a jewel and a feather over the brow, was a typical style but some versions mimicked a Native American chief's war bonnet or a beaded Egyptian headdress.

Right: In this 1926 portrait, the German silent film actress Erna Morena wears a helmet-style headdress with cut-outs.

Below: The Mongol empress Chabi Khatun, consort of Kublai Khan, wears a *boghtaq*, late thirteenth century.

Hats & Bonnets

If protection from the elements was the only purpose served by hats, they would surely have been simple, rather drab affairs with a very broad brim. In fact, throughout history, although women have often used hats to preserve their virtue, they have also used their extraordinary shapes and sizes to establish their position in the social pecking order.

Above: In the first decade of the twentieth century, an American girl tries on the latest hat style in Paris. Such wide-brimmed hats were lampooned by cartoonists.

Right: The Grecian cone hat can be seen in this relief sculpture, c.470 BC.

Grecian Cone Hat

Hats made a rather unlikely debut in ancient Greece when wealthy women wore them perched on their shoulders like tame parakeets. These cone-shaped felt hats with a broad brim appeared to perform no useful function other than to draw attention to one's social status while on the open road.

The Romans also favoured felt hats on occasions but the *pileus*, a brimless felt hat modelled on the Greek cone hat, was worn more conventionally on top of a head of carefully coiffured curls.

Tricorne Hat

Men had long found it convenient to turn up the brims of their hats but in the late seventeenth century it became the fashion to 'cock' it up on three sides, creating the rather dashing tricorne hat. The style actually evolved from the broad-brimmed round hat worn

by Spanish soldiers in Flanders in the seventeenth century. For protection from the constant, soul-destroying Flanders' rain, the French adapted the style by turning the brim up at each of the three corners.

The tricorne was adopted by Peter the Great of Russia, who was keen to bring Western fashions to his Muscovite court, but he wore it over his own hair rather than perched precariously on top of a wig. The style-conscious Louis XIV of France saw the opportunity to cut a dash, so it was soon being worn trimmed with gold or silver lace and waving plumes – and contributing to the romantic image of French musketeers.

In civilian life, the dedicated follower of fashion found it impossible to balance the tricorne on his wig; instead he used it as a stylish 'prop' to make grand gestures to an admiring audience.

Below: A French soldier wearing a tricorne hat. The turned up side brim acted like a gutter, directing the rain away from the wearer's face.

For Liberty

After the Reign of Terror during the French Revolution, any connection to the millinery excesses of the royal court – where the elite had been known to wear hats on top of their bonnets – were abandoned in the desperate resolve to keep one's head. Although simplicity of dress *à la grecque* was the order of the day, to celebrate liberation from the decadence of the *ancien regime*, women still wore headdresses sprouting tall, brightly coloured feathers.

Poke Bonnets

The poke bonnet first became popular in the early nineteenth century when women, dressed in their flimsy Empire gowns, seemed intent on hiding their faces – or possibly their blushes – as some critics of the style remarked.

Also called the 'poking' bonnet, it featured a small crown and long scooping sides, and was tied under the chin with ribbons, allowing the wearer to push her hair inside. Made from velvet in winter and straw in summer, or inexpensive bonnet board when straw was in short supply, the bonnet was generously trimmed with flowers, ribbons and frills. A veil draped over the brim, to protect the wearer's face against the sun, made doubly sure the face was concealed.

The poke bonnet reappeared in the late 1830s when the extravagantly decorated hats of the previous decade, which had lifted away from the face, were now primly tied with ribbons under the chin. Worn close to the head with either a tall crown in a shape sometimes unkindly described as an upturned wastepaper basket, or with a low crown shaped rather like a coal scuttle, it meant a woman's eyes were downcast once more. When she was viewed from the side, only the merest tip of her nose could be seen.

Nineteenth-Century Monstrosities

Hats were so extravagantly decorated in the 1820s and again in the second half of the nineteenth century that they became a veritable hazard to both the

wearer and her unfortunate companion as they struggled to see through clumps of wildly waving ostrich feathers and 'nests' of taxidermed birds.

The modest bonnet, popular in the early years of the nineteenth century, had grown out of all recognition by the 1820s and was festooned with flowers, ears of corn, cascading ribbons and huge bows sticking out in all directions. Ostrich feathers waved above hats worn to the theatre or opera, completely blocking the view of anyone unlucky enough to be sitting behind. In 1826, *La Belle Assemble* described the hats as 'monstrous', deploring the way 'the puffings of silk and ribbon add to their dimension'. By 1829, these decorative monstrosities began to disappear, and when the ribbons were attached to the *inside* rather than the outside of the brim, the hat was on the way to becoming a sensible bonnet again.

Mob Caps

Eventually called mob caps because the poor women who joined the riots in the French Revolution wore them, these cloth bonnets, with a caul that covered the hair and an often frilled or pleated brim, were designed to be worn at home, or under a hat. They remained in use until the twentieth century.

Opposite top: These exaggerated poke bonnet styles look like elongated coal shuttles.

Opposite bottom, above and right: The simpler female attire became in the Regency period, the more elaborate the hat styles. Many were made with leghorn straw, a variety of wheat that was dried and bleached.

Le Petit Journal

ADMINISTRATION
61, RUE LAFAYETTE, 61

Les manuscrits ne sont pas rendus

On s'abonne sans frais
dans tous les bureaux de poste.

5 CENT. SUPPLÉMENT ILLUSTRÉ 5 CENT

22 me Année — Numéro 1.070

ABONNEMENTS

SEINE et SEINE-ET-OISE .. 2 fr. 3 fr. 50
DÉPARTEMENTS .... 2 fr. 4 fr. »
ÉTRANGER .... 2 50 6 fr. »

DIMANCHE 21 MAI 1911

LA MODE A SES DANGERS
Un épervier s'abat sur une élégante dont le chapeau s'ornait d'un pigeon empaillé

Left: The unforeseen perils of fashion – an optimistic sparrowhawk swoops down on a stuffed pigeon adorning a woman's hat, 1911.

Taxidermed Hats

During the second half of the nineteenth century, a bizarre fashion fad grew out of the commercial success of taxidermy. Hat decorations that began as a single feather in the 1860s evolved into an entire stuffed bird in a bucolic setting of leaves, twigs and moss.

A hat without feathers was now barely considered a hat, and no bird was safe from predatory milliners. Egrets, herons and other spectacular species were the prime targets, but death came to even tiny finches. Great care was taken, however, to make sure they were properly wired so they appeared to move on the hat in a 'natural' way!

Driven to Extinction

A profitable plumage trade grew up in London and spread to North America, where at least five million birds were sacrificed on the altar of fashion, pushing some species to the edge of

Mad as a Hatter

Turning animal fur into felt to make hats involved soaking the fur in a solution of mercury nitrate. But inhaling the mercury over long periods had a lethal effect on the hatters, who often developed a form of dementia, earning them the undeserved soubriquet 'mad as a hatter'. Lewis Carroll humorously depicts the Mad Hatter's Tea Party in *Alice in Wonderland*, but it is an all too literal interpretation of a deadly industrial disease that had been identified long before.

extinction. On a walk through New York's Manhattan in 1886, ornithologist Frank Chapman spotted forty species of bird – including a scissor-tailed shrike, a bohemian waxwing and a brown thrasher – all sprouting from hats. In the wild, bird populations were plummeting. When the white egrets, whose feathers were much prized, nearly disappeared from the American South, the hunters moved north to shoot terns and gulls. At the height of the trade, the feathers were worth more than twice their weight in gold.

A few concerned citizens banded together against what they called the demands of a 'barbarous fashion in millinery' and, by 1913, US state and federal laws outlawed what was known as the 'plume trade'. In 1921 the British parliament finally followed suit and imposed a ban after the sober styles of World War I finally brought to an end the reckless use of plumage in the millinery trade.

Below: A fur hat trimmed with feathers by John Frederics, 1939.

Toques
to Turbans

The wildly creative milliner will always find a few daring women to wear the more outlandish styles, especially if the occasion is a royal wedding, but in modern times women's hats have been characterised by relatively simple, clean lines, from the head-hugging cloche and blinker to the wide-brimmed sun hat.

Above: Small feathered hats complement the long, simple silhouette of fashionable French day wear just before the outbreak of World War I.

The Cloche

After the Edwardian period, when the fashionable 'S' shape meant that large hats played their part by tilting forwards over hair piled high, hats began to be 'downsized' significantly. As short hair became fashionable, small close-fitting hats became popular, with the *cloche* hat *the* signature style of the 1920s and '30s. Deep in the crown and often brimless, with a feather at the side, it was pulled down over the forehead. While it could be worn with elegance by those blessed with regular features, it was an unforgiving style that could look like a military helmet on those less fortunate.

Toques decorated with flowers, draped turbans, berets, Russian 'Cossack' hats and pillboxes were all styles seen in the years leading up to World War II. As the hat was the only item of clothing not rationed during the war years, in both the United States and Europe there was a flowering of bright concoctions – frothy creations made of feathers, silk flowers and veils, a cheerful relief from the dreary utility fashions of the time. 'Victory styles', including tiny pillboxes called 'doll's hats', appeared at the end of the war. An American milliner even designed a 'V for Victory' wool turban that was trimmed with rhinestones.

The 1950s was to mark the beginning of the decline in hat wearing, and the headscarf, reminiscent of the very earliest of head coverings, was adopted as an entirely classless fashion. The advent of the youth culture of the 1960s, when hats were scorned unless they were the large floppy 'shepherdess' type, meant many milliners went out of business. But by the last decades of the twentieth century the most

The Blinker and the Breton

Between the wars, fashion reflected the changing role of women, who joined the workforce in droves and affected a boyish silhouette, flattening their breasts and wearing drop-waisted dresses. Their hats, designed to complement their short, permed hairstyles, were held in place with hairpins.

The blinker, usually a close-fitting hat with a small brim worn at a rakish angle, might be in ribbon-decorated straw for day or in sequin-adorned organza for night, while the Breton, a domed straw hat with an upturned brim, could be interpreted into a saucy little adornment, laden with tropical fruit and flowers, which perched over one eye.

Below: A demure Mia Farrow, in an episode of the 1960s television serial *Peyton Place*, wears a Breton hat in ribbon-trimmed straw.

innovative hat-makers were back on the scene, reinventing the fascinator and letting their imaginations run riot, persuading fashionable women that the must-have accessory with guaranteed impact was still, of course, a hat!

Above: With the snugly fitting cloche hat – a practical choice for punting – sitting low on the forehead, women highlighted their eyes and lips with makeup.

In the 1960s, when
informality ruled,
an eye-catching hat
was usually seen only
on special occasions,
such as weddings or
a day at the races.

Above right: The German actress Brigitte Helm
in a silk turban, in the film *Alraune* (1928).

Left: Tania Mallet, who played Tilly Masterson in
the James Bond film *Goldfinger*, in a stiffened net
picture hat by Madame Paulette, 1963.

Right: At the other end of the scale is this
severe, helmet-shaped hat with a bow.

Veils & Cover-Ups

Women have worn veils since ancient times. They can repel and entice attention from lasvicious admirers while at the same time provide even the plainest features with an air of mystery. Nets and caps have long been used to snugly contain the hair but also played an essential role in ensuring no straying lock could offend.

Veils and Wimples

In Anglo-Saxon times, the veil was usually a rectangle of silk or cambric, fastened to one shoulder and draped across the throat and over the head. The circlet of gold that held the veil in place could be worn by women of any class – if they could afford it! Through the centuries the veil has been used for religious observance, as a symbol of virginity in marriage ceremonies and also to conceal the identity of intrepid ladies keeping secret assignations.

The wimple, which originated in the French court in the early thirteenth century, was a length of linen or silk, draped tightly across the throat and under the chin, with the ends pinned to the crown of the head. It may have looked restrictive and uncomfortable, but no doubt it helped women fend off pleurisy and pneumonia in those draughty medieval castles.

Above: The rich red–gold snood in this painting, from about 1530, restrains the girl's hair. In the twenty-first century, a snood is a continuous scarf worn as a hood.

Above left: Need caption

Left: Mary Queen of Scots wears a white mourning wimple, possibly in 1561, the year after the death of her first husband, Francis II of France.

Below: An eighteenth-century satirical illustration of a woman winding on her night cap.

Night Caps

For centuries, simple stocking caps, pulled over the head and onto the neck, provided some desperately needed warmth in inadequately heated dwellings. Men's night caps were traditionally pointed at the end but also acted as a skullcap when they removed their wigs. Women wrapped a long piece of cloth around their heads, which not only kept them warm but also protected styled hair from the ravages of sleep.

Neckwear

The earliest neck cloths were strung rather rakishly around the shoulders of ancient Chinese statuettes, while artefacts from the Roman Empire and Egypt also depict men wearing what seems to be the original version of the necktie. Throughout history neckwear has enjoyed a practical reputation, but the somewhat redundant necktie of the modern era seems in imminent danger of ending up on the remnants table.

Kerchiefs and Couvre-chefs

The kerchief, or *couvre-chef* in French – literally 'cover-the-head' – was a triangular or square piece of material with a number of uses. Worn as early as the sixteenth century, it was tied around either the head to provide protection or the neck for warmth. The kerchief was often impregnated

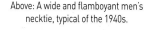

Above: A wide and flamboyant men's necktie, typical of the 1940s.

Right: A kerchief might be made of homespun cloth or fine linen and lace, depending on the wealth of the wearer.

The high collar was at its most lethal when its two triangular points came up so high that they threatened to poke out an eye or two.

with a rose or lavender fragrance so the wearer could dab sweat from the forehead or wave it under the nose to ward off a bad smell.

Croatian Cravats

During the Thirty Years War in the seventeenth century, the traditional small knotted neckerchief worn by Croatian mercenaries serving in the French army became all the rage at the French court. The cravat, which derives from a corrupt French pronunciation of *Hrvat*, the Serbo-Croat word for Croat, was a large square made out of muslin or silk, folded cornerwise into a band and wrapped round the neck in a knot or a bow.

The popularity of the cravat soon spread throughout Europe. By the time it appeared again in the late eighteenth century, the cravat had undergone a transformation – there were at least fourteen different ways to tie it, and fashionable young men were

prepared to spend their mornings finessing its arrangement. Whole books were devoted to this subtle art.

Stiff Collars and Stocks

In the early nineteenth century, elegant young men – or dandies, as they were known – were distinguished not only by the fine cut of their coats but also by their stiff collars. The high collar was at its most lethal when its two triangular points came up so high that they threatened to poke out an eye or two. These points were kept in place by a neck cloth, in the form of either a cravat or what was called a stock – a stiffened neckband buckled behind the neck, which was sometimes so tight a dandy would find it impossible to turn his head.

Neckties

Once the workplaces of the Industrial Revolution demanded hard-wearing neckwear that was easy to put on in the morning, the cravat was replaced by a more convenient modern necktie. In its

original form – usually long, thin and often sombre in colour – the tie was fastened with a knot that would not come undone easily. After World War I, New York tie-makers developed a way of cutting the fabric on the bias and sewing three segments together. Hand-painted ties up to 11.5 cm (4½ in) wide became fashionable among American men but, in England, the Duke of Windsor made regimental ties with stripes popular, the trend outlasting his brief reign as King Edward VIII.

After World War II, ties became wider and even more colourful, providing demobbed soldiers with a chance to celebrate their escape from those necessarily monotonous military uniforms. Ties continued to change shape with each decade, growing thinner and shorter until the 1960s, when they expanded and blossomed with Op Art designs, cartoon characters and joke ties for those keen to flout the buttoned-up look they were required to wear to their nine-to-five jobs.

5
dandies & divas

If you are not in fashion, you are nobody.

EARL OF CHESTERFIELD, 1694–1773

Royal Trendsetters

The first celebrities to flounce along red carpets and have their outfits critiqued and copied were royals. From Madame Pompadour to Princess Diana, from the Sun King to the Duke of Windsor, they have been our arbiters of taste and style, sometimes setting trends that lasted for generations. Even Queen Victoria – never exactly cover girl material – had a powerful impact on the sales of bombazine.

Above: Jeanne Antoinette Poisson, mistress of Louis XV of France, known as Madame de Pompadour or 'Pom-Pom'.

The Sun King

Louis XIV of France, who ruled for an astonishing 72 years, was revered as a 'visible divinity', hence his lofty sobriquet, the Sun King. Although a great patron of the arts, in turn he demanded that artists and writers praised him to the skies on every possible occasion. At war with sensible dressers, particularly Protestants, Louis preferred a wardrobe of pure flounce and frivolity. During his reign the cumbersome pannier-style skirt became the fashion for women (see page 22) and, seemingly to be fair and balanced, men's coats became longer, wider and more awkward, too.

Pom-Pom Poisson

Jeanne Antoinette Poisson was a smart woman, an accomplished musician and actress, and a great beauty. When she showed up at a palace ball in 1745, Louis XV of France didn't stand a chance. Within a month she was his official mistress, with her own apartment in the Palace of Versailles, and a title – Madame de Pompadour.

She loved the delicate translucence of fine porcelain, which she bought by the cartload. With white lead she gave her face a porcelain glaze, added detail with rouge, then wrapped herself in layers and layers of marshmallow softness. She preferred hand-painted silk in rich floral patterns, often sewn with silk flowers and bows, and dripping with ruffles.

Even the great individualist Marie Antoinette was profoundly influenced by Madame de Pompadour a generation later. But her lasting legacy can be appreciated in all the things named after her. Pompadour Pink continued to appear on colour charts until the

Left: A 1670 portrait of Louis XIV of France, often known as the Sun King, whose court remains the gold standard for fashionable extravagance.

Below: The Duchess of Windsor, née Wallis Simpson (left) and her third husband, the Duke of Windsor, who could both cut a stylish swathe, even in Paris.

of prosperity to the Scottish knitting industry. He popularised the Panama hat for sunny days and the snap-brim trilby for cloudy, rainy ones. And he gave his name to the Windsor knot, the Windsor collar (with a wider spread to accommodate the knot), the Prince of Wales collar (wider still) and the toned-down version of Glenurquhart Plaid known as Prince of Wales check. That's dapper.

American socialite Wallis Simpson's wardrobe was so impressive that Edward VIII renounced the British throne for its owner.

Wallis, later the Duchess of Windsor, was someone who knew the importance of being well dressed. As she said herself, 'I'm not a beautiful woman. I'm nothing to look at, so the only thing I can do is dress better than anyone else'. A trendsetter to the end, she reportedly wore a Paco Rabanne space suit to the Duke of Windsor's funeral in 1972.

early twentieth century. High, narrow heels are still sometimes called Pompadour heels, and a high quiff, Elvis-style (see page 214), bears the name 'Pompadour'.

The Duke and Duchess of Windsor

The Duke of Windsor was dapper. He couldn't discharge his royal duties without the woman he loved but, unlike many men of his generation, he *could* choose a shirt on his own. Some of his sartorial innovations were not welcomed, however. During a tour of India, for instance, he acquired a taste for an ankle-high suede sports shoe known as a 'Chukka Boot'. His much-imitated taste for fairisle sweaters as golf wear brought a degree

Macaroni Fops

Fops, coxcombs, popinjays and fashion-mongers will always be with us, but no one can compete with the Macaroni fop. His hair was huge, his clothes were loud and his heels were high, and nobody ever worked a quizzing glass quite like him.

Above: According to *The Oxford Magazine* of 1770, 'There is indeed a kind of animal, neither male nor female, a thing of the neuter gender, lately started up among us'. This 'animal' was the Macaroni fop.

Above left: Such elegance in the Macaroni's dress required great attention to detail.

Left: A caricature containing elements of truth, such as the nosegay and the tiny hat perched on the wig.

Simpering He-She Things

During the eighteenth century, The Grand Tour – a trip around Europe, often with a tutor, known as a 'bear-leader', in tow – was considered an essential part of every wealthy Englishman's upbringing. It was all supposed to be highly educational but, to the dismay of their elders, rather than returning with heads

The marks of a true Macaroni were 'theatrical' mannerisms, a squeaky voice, white breeches, a tight-sleeved, short-skirted jacket, a fancy waistcoat (probably decorated with extravagant buttons or lace), a quizzing glass and very, very big hair.

filled with Treasures of the Renaissance and Classical Ruins, some of these 'spindle-shanked gentry' came back badly affected by 'foreign ways' as 'sweet-scented, simpering, He-she Things'. And because it was assumed that Italy was the main source of corruption, the simpering He-she things were nicknamed 'Macaronis'.

The marks of a true Macaroni were 'theatrical' mannerisms, a squeaky voice, white breeches, a tight-sleeved, short-skirted jacket, a fancy waistcoat (probably decorated with extravagant buttons or lace), a quizzing glass and very, very big hair. Cartoonists went mostly for the hair – depicting wigs, up to a metre (3 ft) high, richly decorated

with curls, a fat ponytail falling to the waist and a tiny tricorn hat balanced on the top.

In an age when sober merchants wore broadcloth suitings in drab colours as a mark of their seriousness, the Macaronis – dressed in pastels, pea green, deep orange, brocaded silks and sequins, and red-heeled slippers with shiny buckles, strewn with a diamond or two – caused some alarm.

A 'Macaroni Club' is often spoken of, although there is some doubt as to whether this was a real place or just a state of mind. The Earl of Chesterfield certainly believed it to be a real place when he issued dire warnings to his godson never to go there.

The word 'Macaroni' acquired flexible usage. It came to mean 'anything fashionable', as in 'Oh, that's very Macaroni'. Excess was implied.

Because of the Macaroni's happy adoption of foreign fashions and customs, the word could also be used to mean 'unpatriotic' or 'traitor', so when an eighteenth-century worthy like Charles James Fox, the anti-slavery campaigner and supporter of the French Revolution, is described as a 'Macaroni', as he often was, it's hard to know whether he had big hair, liked foreigners or whether it was just some homophobic slur. His portraits, showing a portly gent soberly dressed, make the big hair slur seem unlikely.

Buttons & Beaux

In tailors' cutting rooms and at shirtmakers' presses, certain names are spoken of in hushed, reverent tones. These are the names of the great dandies – the heroes of fashion, the memory of whose cut, drape, balance and taper live on long after the worm has devoured their bodies and the moth their suits. 'Every faculty of his soul, spirit, person and purse,' said Thomas Carlyle in his description of the dandy, 'is heroically consecrated to this one object – the wearing of clothes, wisely and well'.

Above: An 1805 portrait of George 'Beau' Brummell, whose understated elegance was partly a reaction to the absurd excesses of Macaroni style.

Brummell, Prince of Trousers

In 1795, the British government put a tax on hair powder, which had been used for years to keep gentlemen's wigs white (see page 211). The tax was not a success. Wigs quickly went out of fashion, not only because of the tax but also because Beau Brummell, the trendiest trendsetter in the history of trendsetting, did not wear one.

George 'Beau' Brummell inherited a fortune while he was still in his teens, set up house in London, and found himself hanging with the in-crowd – the in-crowd at that time being the select group of young men who were allowed to call George, Prince of Wales, 'Prinny'.

Although certainly a dandy, Beau Brummell was not a fancy dresser. The Macaronis of a generation before, bedecked in their sudden colours and disquieting patterns, would have written him off as a monochrome dullard fit only for a funeral. But it was he who established the basics of what was to become 'the English gentleman's style' for the next 150 years. In effect, he single-handedly wrote the rules which are still followed today in London's Savile Row and Jermyn Street.

Brummel used only the finest tailors of the day and was so particular that it is said he commissioned one tailor to make the fingers of his kid gloves and another the thumbs.

Overnight, gaudiness and ostentation became undignified. A gentleman should be judged by his grooming, the perfect cut of his clothes and the quality of the fabric – always in muted tones. And Brummell also broke with centuries-old traditions by bathing every day. He shaved. He brushed his teeth. His shirt was always snow-white. And, perhaps most radical of all his reforms, in an age

when knee breeches and stockings were still the norm, he wore trousers, usually tucked into his canvas boots, but unmistakably trousers.

This ensemble of jacket, trousers, waistcoat, shirt and tie – or, in his case, cravat – is still standard office wear for men in most parts of the world although, unlike Beau Brummell, few modern office workers polish their shoes with champagne.

Above: Every generation has its own version of the dandy. In London in 1967 he might have shopped at I Was Lord Kitchener's Valet on Portobello Road.

Left: A dandy checking the cut of a new coat, from a nineteenth-century lithograph.

Asked how much it cost to dress this well, Brummell replied, 'Why, with tolerable economy, I think it might be done with £800'. In modern terms, it cost him perhaps a million dollars.

Brummell transformed dressing into an art form. He was rumoured to take up to five hours to get ready, and an audience of other dandies came to watch the perfomance. There must have been little time for Brummell to be out of the house as he spent hours dressing in the morning and then undressing again in the afternoon, only to dress once again for the evening.

In the end it was gambling more than tailor's bills that caused him to flee the country, pursued by creditors. That, and calling his former friend the Prince of Wales 'fat'. He spent the rest of his life in France, and died in a lunatic asylum, dressed in rags and lying on straw.

dandies & divas 137

Left: Charles Baudelaire (1821–1867), in understated, but always smart, black.

Opposite: As Oscar Wilde (pictured) writes in his novel, *The Picture of Dorian Gray*: 'Those who find beautiful meanings in beautiful things are the cultivated. For these there is hope.'

latest voguish colour as 'the new black', in a sense they are harking back to Baudelaire, the original 'man in black', who made it the ultimate fashion colour to which all others must be compared.

The Importance of Being Oscar

'One should either be a work of art, or wear a work of art', said Oscar Wilde. At the age of 13, Oscar was writing to his mother from school, asking for shirts in scarlet and lilac. Wilde was an early convert to Aestheticism, a movement that, under the banner 'Art for Art's Sake', believed that beauty was an end in itself and should be sought in one's surroundings, in one's reading, in one's thoughts and, perhaps most of all, in oneself.

The Aesthetics shared some of the aims of the Victorian Dress Reform movement, in as much as they were anti-corset but, whereas the Reformers wanted to run, jump and play tennis, the Aesthetics smiled superciliously at any suggestion that clothes should be practical or, worse, sporty.

Oscar, 100 years after they'd gone out of fashion, adopted knee breeches and stockings and wore ribbons in his little leather slippers. His jackets were rich velvet. His colours of choice were claret, chartreuse, perhaps a shocking splash of yellow and, following his firm belief that 'a well-tied tie is the first serious step in life', he took the same level of care with his neckwear as Michelangelo did with the Sistine Chapel.

Like Brummell and Baudelaire, the world did not treat Oscar well. At the age of 40, he was imprisoned for 'gross indecency' and did two years' hard labour. Three years after his release, he died in a French hotel room declaring, 'Either that wallpaper goes, or I do'.

> The dandy must aspire to be sublime without interruption; he must live and sleep before a mirror.

'Beau-delaire'

The French symbolist poet Charles Baudelaire regarded dandyism as more important than the mere choosing of a tie or the lacing of a shoe. Dandyism was a philosophy. The dandy's sole profession, he said, should be elegance. 'The dandy must aspire to be sublime without interruption; he must live and sleep before a mirror.'

Yet his taste was even more austere than Beau Brummell's. Dandyism, he believed, should value perfect simplicity above all else. He favoured black – the colour of absence, the colour of death, the colour of night, of perfect elegance. When fashion writers describe the

Quaintrelles

On one level a quaintrelle is just your basic high-maintenance diva. But on another level she is a living work of art, a woman who expresses her passion through her appearance and surroundings, a woman who thinks nothing of fashion but thinks everything of style – in other words, a high-maintenance diva.

Above: The sometimes androgynous Marlene Dietrich in top hat and tails, 1929.

Left: Influential French couturier Coco Chanel, 1936, her neck swathed in her signature pearls.

The Duchess

Two hundred years before her great-great grandniece Princess Diana was gracing the cover of almost every magazine on the planet, Georgiana Cavendish, the Duchess of Devonshire, was the fashion plate of her day. Invited to almost every party of consequence, Georgiana was at the forefront of fashion. Fine ladies everywhere followed in her wake and if the Duchess wore a hat adorned with artificial fruit or a ship in full sail, or a muslin dress with silver sprigs, you can be sure that the fine ladies would be doing the same in record time.

A Firm Hand-Snake

An extreme example of this extreme genus was the extraordinary Luisa, Marquise Casati Stampa di Soncino. She liked to wear live snakes as bracelets and, completely naked under a fur coat, also liked to take out her pet cheetahs, on diamond-studded chains, for an evening stroll.

Although born to money, debt overtook her and towards the end she could sometimes be seen in the streets of London, scrabbling through bins in search of feathers to decorate her hair. Wearing false eyelashes and a leopard-skin coat and trousers, she was buried with her beloved Pekingese dogs. The artist Augustus John thought it was a waste: 'She should have been shot, stuffed and displayed in a glass case'.

Cara Tamara

The Polish-born artist Tamara de Lempicka was a great beauty. In her paintings of herself she is a woman of heroic glamour. In a 1929 painting entitled *Self-Portrait in a Green Bugatti*, Tamara is in billowing yellow, helmeted

Above: A Gainsborough portrait of Georgiana, Duchess of Devonshire, c.1785–87, who wears the famous 'portrait' or 'Gainsborough' hat, one of her trend-setting accessories.

Left: Tamara de Lempicka, in a dress with pleated frills by Marcel Rochas, c.1931.

and be–gloved, a Jazz Age woman, staring out with cold and rapacious eyes from behind the wheel of a monster car. Her scarf flows like water, filling the passenger seat. Two years earlier the dancer Isadora Duncan had been strangled when her scarf caught in the wheel of a green Bugatti, but Quaintrelles were never slaves to health and safety.

Coco Chanel

The French couturier Gabrielle 'Coco' Chanel is undoubtedly one of the best known quaintrelles. She introduced the concept of simple, yet expensive, clothing for women, such as the Chanel suit and the 'little black dress'. She was also said to have 'genius, lethal wit, sarcasm and maniacal destructiveness, which intrigued and appalled everyone'.

Chanel mixed with the *crème de la crème* of society, had a relationship with composer Igor Stravinsky, and was even a Nazi spy during World War II.

Above: Audrey Hepburn is remembered for Givenchy's 'spare style', epitomised by simple but elegant sheath dresses in beautiful fabrics.

Left: Grace Kelly, who became the Princess of Monaco, wearing a grey silk dress. Many of her on-screen costumes were designed by the legendary Edith Head.

Falling in Love with Marlene

From the cabaret clubs and theatres of 1920s Berlin there emerged a woman whose magnetism sent shock waves through Berlin, Paris, London, New York and Hollywood. Marlene Dietrich was never the girl next door; or, if she was, you were in a suite at the Ritz.

Her look was strangely androgynous. Like the male impersonators of music hall and variety, she appreciated the sexual edge to be gained from teaming a top hat and tuxedo with a burning cigarette in a long holder and little else. It is said that when Marlene strode purposefully up the Champs-Élysées in the spring of 1933, men abandoned their cars and left their café tables to follow her up the street.

She took nothing for granted. Glamour, in her book, was not something you

Right: Marlene Dietrich, who could carry off wearing a man's suit or a skin-tight gown that made her look naked under thousands of sequins.

possess but something you worked for – and she worked very hard.

When she travelled, Marlene took a mountain of luggage and cleaned her hotel rooms with chloroform. At Paris couture houses she made the seamstresses rip up seams until she was satisfied with the fit of a garment, and had glovemakers pin and repin gloves on her hand to get a perfect fit.

Her dedication to her appearance always superseded her talent for acting; one reviewer called her a 'monosyllabic clotheshorse'.

In her later years, fabulously dressed and with her flesh meticulously enhanced by surgical tape and other procedures, Marlene gave cabaret performances, growling her hits. After one of her performances, a lover maliciously compared watching her undress to watching 'a mummy being unwound'. But most worshipped her. Her only daughter marvelled at Marlene's ability to objectify herself; her ability to see herself as 'a thing, a superior product, to be constantly scrutinised for the slightest imperfection'. And until her death in 1992 that's how her fans saw her too.

Grace and Audrey

There is some discussion as to what exactly makes a quaintrelle, but the term derives from the French word *cointe* (related to quaint), meaning 'cunningly devised'. A quaintrelle knows how to dress for effect, and has her own personal, often quirky style.

American film star Audrey Hepburn was the first to make the gamine and waif look fashionable and she eventually became a muse for couturier, Givenchy. Her chic looks from the films *Roman Holiday* (1953) and *Breakfast at Tiffany's*

(1961) are still much copied today, and are considered the height of good style.

Another film star to create an iconic look was American Grace Kelly. Life certainly imitated art as during filming for *The Swan* (1956) – where she played the role of a young aristocratic girl who becomes a princess – in real life she had begun seeing Monaco's Prince Rainer, whom she was later to marry and herself become a princess.

When Marlene strode purposefully up the Champs-Élysées...men abandoned their cars and left their café tables to follow her up the street.

Romantics
Old & New

Romanticism was an eighteenth-century movement created to rebel against the sensible Age of Reason and to revere the natural world and all things wild. However, it is wise, when you're wearing a floppy shirt with long lacy cuffs, to be wary of moving parts; which is perhaps one of the reasons Romantics have always preferred wild but snag-free nature to the machine age.

Above: Percy Bysshe Shelley and his future wife Mary Godwin, both prominent writers of the Romantic movement.

Mad, Bad and Dangerous to Know

The Romantics were proto-Goths who preferred mountains, storms and ghosts to reason, tea time and cotton mills, and often took drugs. The poster boy of this set was of course the poet George, Lord Byron.

George loved dressing up and having his portrait painted. He was painted in Albanian traditional dress – a dark crimson jacket, flamboyant turban of scarlet and green, gold-work cloak (see right). He was painted in burgundy velvet and a gold-tipped muslin shirt. He was painted in a rose-coloured satin robe over a soft linen shirt with a large floppy collar held together with a ruby brooch. If it was sumptuous, oriental and exotic, George wanted to be painted wearing it.

Where George 'Beau' Brummell (see page 136) had favoured smooth, tight neatness, the Romantics saw 'loose' as being more in keeping with their general preoccupation with passion, freedom and the untrammelled imagination. Their shirts were fuller, with tucked inserts on the chest and flowing sleeves. Cravats were more fluid and graceful. The starved look was admired, so shoulders were padded big and broad to emphasise the small waist.

The Romantics borrowed freely from other times and other cultures. *Ferronières* – jewelled headbands worn across the forehead – made the odd appearance, and there was much reliance on lacy ruffs and heavy brocades. But Romantics rarely made old bones. John Keats died at 25, Percy Bysshe Shelley at 29 and Byron at 36. When they went, the Romance withered and, by 1840, attitudes and clothes were again tightly buttoned.

A Wild Nobility

Nearly 150 years after Byron doffed his first turban, British designer Vivienne Westwood's 'Pirates' collection of 1981 kick-started a New Romantic movement. It was a reaction to the stark and confrontational style of the Punks, and revelled in the frills and flamboyant fabrics that the long-dead poets and aesthetes rejoiced in.

And like the Old Romantics, this new breed revelled in the old and the exotic, cherry-picking influences from Russian Constructivism, circus clowns, Scottish Baronialism and David Bowie. This eclecticism also dragged in warpaint from Native Americans, hats and jackets from highwaymen, roll-top boots, pigtails and kerchiefs from pirates. Floppy shirts were ubiquitous, and everybody wore lots of makeup.

The 1980s nightclub scene – first in London and then the world – was soon overtaken by swashbuckling rakes,

Above: Ever a fan of dress-ups, especially if it involved velvet and gold brocade, Lord Byron poses for his portrait in traditional Albanian dress, 1813.

Right: Byron might have envied Adam Ant's costume, an improbable combination of hussar jacket, black leather trousers, belts, scarves, feathers and warpaint.

gilded dandies, consumptive maidens and unhinged buccaneers. The New Romantic movement was nothing if not androgynous, and sometimes the consumptive maidens were men and sometimes the swashbuckling dandies were women.

In the 1990s Alexander McQueen, *l'enfant terrible* of British fashion,

revived the revival briefly with his flamboyant three-point origami frockcoats, exaggerated silhouettes and melancholic sheer lace blouses, although what Lord Byron's reaction would have been to McQueen's infamous 'Bumsters' – that's right, trousers with the buttocks cut out of them – can only be imagined.

Spaced Out

American astronaut John Glenn's orbit of the earth in 1963 sent couturiers on Earth into a spin. Silver and PVC space suits became de rigueur on the catwalks, with designers such as André Courrèges being among the first to seek out new frontiers in 1964, followed closely by Pierre Cardin, Paco Rabanne and Rudi Gernreich. Hats with visors and clothing made from plastics and metals were fused with geometric designs and colours taken from the prevalent Op Art style of the day, in primary reds, blues and yellows teamed with white, black and silver.

To Boldly Go-Go

In the early 1960s, the world's anxieties about the Cold War, atomic bombs and space exploration filtered through into the world of fashion and resulted in ultra-modern 'protective'-style gear – all-in-one suits with boots, gloves, helmets and goggles with tiny slits for the eyes, that all looked impervious to impending atomic disaster. Cybernetic visions of the future also had an impact on fashion, with an almost robot-like look appearing in clear Plexiglas bubble helmets and visors.

The simultaneous explosion of synthetics had designers leaping at the new futuristic fabrics, such as PVC, polyester and other acrylics. Former civil engineer and designer Paco Rabanne incorporated plastics, metals and chain-mail into his looks. He strung together small discs or squares of plastic to create mini-length tunics.

Above left: American actress Raquel Welch in a futuristic outfit, featuring electric blue PVC skirt and scarf with a perspex visor, c.1967.

Above: Models Celia Hammond and Pattie Boyd wear 'Capsule' felt helmets with dots and moons, created by designer Edward Mann, c.1965.

Left: Silver 'Cosmocorps' designs by Pierre Cardin, showing his trademark unisex style, 1968.

Below: A Braniff Airways air hostess in the clear Plexiglass helmet known as the 'space bubble' designed by Emilio Pucci, 1965.

The Op Art movement of the 1960s, led by artists such as Victor Vasarely and Bridget Riley, was also a great influence on fashions of the time, with these black and white and primary abstract images working perfectly with the minimalist shapes of the new, post-modern space age fashion.

Simple shift dresses were popular, in primary yellows, reds and blues, often with bold geometric designs, such as circles or stripes. Pants with go-faster stripes down the sides were also seen and what we now think of as the 1960s 'go-go boot' was really the space boot style from this fashion wave.

Apollo Moon Landings

However, the cosmic dust didn't really settle on ordinary earthlings until after 1968 with the smash hit sci-fi movie *Barbarella* and all the excitement about the Apollo moon landings. Paco Rabanne and Jacques Fonteray designed the costumes for the movie and the glorious, figure-hugging catsuit was born. It became popular in the mainstream, not just for women, but also for men and even children too, looking its best tucked into a pair of space boots, worn with a wide, often low-slung, belt that looked ideal for holstering a ray-gun.

The Braniff Space Bubble

When the Italian designer Emilio Pucci was commissioned to design air hostess uniforms for Braniff International Airways – the makers of Concorde – he made costumes fit for the Earth–Mars Shuttle, putting each luckless hostess ('Tea or coffee, Sir?') into a transparent space helmet called a 'space bubble', two-colour go-go boots, lime gloves and a reversible coat.

Cybernetic visions of the future also had an impact on fashion, with an almost robot-like look appearing in clear Plexiglas bubble helmets and visors.

Tribes

The tribal instinct runs deep. A tribe can be your extended family, your security, your identity. While once the question was, 'Are you a Catholic or a Protestant?', in the 1960s the question was 'Are you a Mod or a Rocker?'. Tribes or subcultures, largely identified by their fashions, were prevalent in the twentieth century, from the Zoot Suits of the Harlem Renaissance to the 'ankle-freezers' and skinny ties of the 1960s Mod.

Above: the typical shift-style dresses of the 1960s Mod style, with their strong geometric designs, probably made from synthetic fabric such as Crimplene.

Right: Three young Jamaican men wearing Zoot Suits, 1948.

Zooted and Booted

'A killer-diller coat with a drape shape, reet pleats and shoulders padded like a lunatic's cell', was how one wearer described his Zoot Suit. Teamed with wide-topped, narrow-bottomed, high-waisted trousers, a broad-brimmed felt, pointed 'French' shoes, a flat-top haircut, a spear-point collar and a mouthful of jive-talk, Zoot style, in one form or another, remained the 'righteous' way for disaffected youth from the late-1930s to the mid-1950s.

The 'Harlem Renaissance' of the 1930s brought a new sense of dignity and identity to African-Americans. The extravagant, loose cut of the Zoot, which first appeared at this time, matched the pride and the vibe. And on the dance floor the fabric flailed.

Teddy Boys

With a nod to the dandies of the Edwardian period, the cult of the Teddy Boy ('Teddy' being short for Edward) started to gain prominence across

Britain during the 1950s. Teddy Boys, who were anything but cuddly – being partial to a bit of violence and destruction – donned long jackets ('drape coats'), high-waisted 'drain pipe' trousers, 'slim Jim' ties and fancy brocaded waistcoats.

He's a Mod

Unlike their rivals the Rockers, who wore leather jackets and rode motor bikes, emulating the fashionable American working man's look of Marlon Brando and James Dean, Mods took their lead from American Ivy League fashions and the suave Italian look. Cars and motorbikes were rejected in favour of shiny Italian Vespa and Lambretta motor scooters.

A Mod's typical outfit was a suit with a short ('bum-freezer') jacket, which he teamed with immaculate white shirts, narrow ties, straight-legged pants that exposed the ankle ('ankle-freezers') and winkle-pickers (see page 70).

Gone were the dull short-back-and-side haircuts and the 'French crew' became all the rage, and Mods were certainly not averse to a bit of backcombing, too – while tapping their feet to the beat of soul, blues and British power pop.

Although Mod was very much the domain of the dandified 1960s male, Mary Quant shanghaied the Mod look for girls with miniskirts and geometric hairstyles such as the bob.

The Mod look became popular again in the 1980s during the post-Punk phase, when youth and fashion subcultures such as New Romantics, Rude Boys and Rockabillies abounded.

Above: High fashion celebrated the bohemian style of the Hippy movement, although real hippies tended to wear jeans and an Indian shirt.

Right: An all-white outfit for him and a miniskirt in a psychedelic pattern for her, c.1968.

Peace, Flowers and Freedom

It started with a philosophy. A way of entirely reorganising the world so that, without coercion, people would renounce their materialistic, consumerist, violent ways and free their spirits. Starting as a chummier wing of the Beatnik movement, in America the Hippy tribe flourished as a non-confrontational opposition movement to the escalating Vietnam War and, from there, spread throughout the world.

As far as clothes went, anything would do as long as it was cheap or free. Much Hippy clothing was self-made or customised, bought from flea markets or secondhand shops. Jeans were bell-bottomed by opening the side seams and inserting inverted V-shaped pieces of velvet or brocade. Fringes and beads were allowed to sprout on waistcoats and skirts. T-shirts and dresses were tie-dyed or batiked in psychedelic colours.

During the Summer of Love in 1967, the Western world exploded with kaftans, beads, body paint and the pungent reek of Afghan coats. Then it all went wrong.

Underwear became optional and hemlines either rose to the waist or dropped to the floor. Knee length probably meant you were a police spy.

Later these styles were mixed with ethnic influences. The Hippies knew which side they were on in the Cowboys versus Indians grudge match, so they adopted Native American beadwork and traditional decorations.

During the Summer of Love in 1967, the Western world exploded with kaftans, beads, body paint and the pungent reek of Afghan coats. Then it all went wrong. By the beginning of the 1970s, 'Hippy' had broken out of the tribe and become the prevalent style for most under-25s (as well as older folk who fancied themselves) on at least four continents. The big manufacturers saw the new demographic and rubbed their hands.

Jeans didn't just come in blue anymore, and neither did they have

In the mid-1970s Punk, the quintessential youth movement of rebellion, pushed its way into the world kicking and screaming.

to be denim. They were blue, orange, plum, lime, paisley, embroidered and appliquéd, and made of velvet – plain or crushed – corduroy, suede and sailcloth. Chain store shirts came in colours, too, and in patterns other than a discreet stripe. Cost accountants grew their hair and took to wearing huge floral ties. Suits – even politician's suits – sprouted flares. Teachers wore kaftans to work and the world drowned in cheesecloth. Luckily by this time the original Hippies, for whom it had all meant so much more, couldn't remember anything before last Tuesday.

All the Young Punks

In the mid-1970s Punk, the quintessential youth movement of rebellion, pushed its way into the world kicking and screaming.

The soundtrack of Punk was provided by American bands like The Ramones and British bands such as The Sex Pistols and The Clash, and the members of these bands became the fashion inspiration for millions of dispirited youths worldwide.

The favoured American Punk ensemble was the 1950s look of t-shirt, leather jacket and jeans, firmly entrenching this as *the* cool look for dudes and rockstars

forever after. However, in Britain, fashion designer Vivienne Westwood and her partner Malcolm McLaren had much to do with creating the archetypal Punk look of 'destroy' t-shirts (pre-ripped and befouled, often with antisocial imagery such as swastikas), bondage-style clothing, leather jackets with spikes and studs, clothing made from garbage bags and the use of safety pins as decoration and jewellery.

Below: Three young Punks in Stockholm, 1977. The safety pin through the cheek was one of the more hard-core looks of the Punk subculture..

If you weren't a Hippy in the 1960s, you might have been wearing day dresses like these – simple sheaths, often in bold geometric blocks of colour, like the one British singer Cilla Black wears (right) or opposite.

The 'Dress Hoop-La-La' (below), featuring cutouts around the midriff, is teamed with a helmet-style hat.

The Op Art movement of the 1960s, led by artists such as Victor Vasarely and Bridget Riley, was also a great influence on fashions of the time with these black and white and primary abstract images working perfectly with the minimalist shapes…

6
greasepaint & powder

Women have two weapons – cosmetics and tears. SAMUEL JOHNSON, 1709–1784

Lovely Smells & *Bathing* Belles

'Bath twice a day to be really clean,' English novelist Anthony Burgess said, 'once a day to be passably clean, and once a week to avoid being a public menace'. Avoiding public menace is a key characteristic of civilised behaviour. This is why all the truly great civilisations have set such great store by a good long soak, ideally in something with an agreeable smell followed by a discreet dab or two of something with an even more agreeable smell. Here's how some of the greatest civilisations have followed the primrose path to the long, hot bath.

Secrets of the Perfumier

In ancient Egypt cleanliness was close to godliness. Smelly people, the Egyptians believed, would not be received into the afterlife. Even the process of mummification was partly devised so a corpse would continue to delight the nose for all eternity.

The Egyptians wore wigs with flowing hairstyles, and their wearers depilated obsessively – head, armpits, chest, legs, genitals, back – by either shaving or tweezing. Then they'd wash, either at home or in the river, and finally anoint themselves liberally with scented oils and unguents – their moisturiser, a rice bran-based sunblock and deodorant.

Some of the perfumes they used must have cost a fortune. Frankincense probably had to be transported all the way from the Horn of Africa, and myrrh from Arabia. Although white lily and lotus were grown locally, jasmine and narcissus were imported from India.

Smell was sacred, and each god had his or her own perfume. The art of the perfumier was a holy secret, initially practised only by priests and only in the temple. They had their work cut out. At one point a law was passed commanding all citizens to perfume themselves at least once a week, and at parties it was common to put on the head of guests a little cone of perfumed tallow, which would melt as the evening wore on, anointing the face, neck and shoulders. An export market opened up too. When priestly production could no

Above left: A Corinthian aryballos, a small flask that was used to store perfume or oil, 500 BC.

Left: Ambergris, secreted by a whale's intestines and found floating on the sea or washed up on the shore, is still used as a perfume fixative, although it has largely been replaced by synthetic substitutes.

Showered with Perfume

By I AD, Rome was getting through 2540 tonnes of frankincense a year and 500 tonnes of myrrh. Nero, emperor at the time, blew the price of a house on perfume for a single party – it showered on his guests from special nozzles in the ceiling. Meanwhile cavities in the walls threw out clouds of rose petals so dense that one guest died of asphyxiation. This was not a religious celebration or ritual. Perfume had become what it has been ever since – sex in a bottle.

Left: The implied Eastern influence in this 1914 Art Nouveau advertisement reflects the fact that Islamic cultures refined the art of perfume-making.

Below: A Lalique perfume bottle, the stopper adorned with a figure of Amphitrite – in Greek mythology, a sea goddess and wife of Poseidon.

longer keep up with demand, factories were opened, but still the trade secrets were jealously guarded.

Egyptian reverence for smell was shared by other cultures. The Mosaic law of the Jews, for instance, banned the use of many perfumes for secular use. When the Song of Solomon compares the 'well-beloved' to 'a bundle of myrrh' and a 'cluster of camphire', it's not just being racy, it's verging on blasphemy.

Other cultures, however, failed to appreciate the spiritual nuances. Kyphi was an incense made of cinnamon, cedar, honey and myrrh. In Egypt it was restricted to religious purposes, but the Greeks set the tone for the rest of history by using it as an aphrodisiac.

Above: For wealthy Roman women, pale skin with a healthy pink blush to the cheeks was fashionable. The rouge might be achieved with rose and poppy petals or crocodile dung, and any blemishes could be covered with a soft leather patch, the ancient forerunner of the *mouche* (see page 165).

Above right: A Roman woman pours perfume into a phial, first century AD. The Romans used different perfumes for different purposes – from anointing the soles of one's feet (and the family pet) to showering triumphant legions after a successful campaign.

A Day at the Baths

The ancient Greeks had nothing against bathing. Small bathtubs, washbasins and so on were common features in Greek homes. Keeping clean, they believed, was a minor but nonetheless worthwhile feature of the civilised life.

Most Romans, on the other hand, reckoned that bathing was civilisation itself, or at least its finest achievement. 'The gong that announced the opening of the public baths,' wrote the poet Cicero, 'was a sweeter sound than the voices of all the philosophers'. By 354 AD, Rome had nearly a thousand bathhouses. The biggest, the Baths of Diocletian, had facilities for 3000.

A good bathhouse served the functions of health club, community centre, massage parlour, manicurist, casino – and in some cases theatre, sports arena, concert hall, bar, restaurant, library and brothel. Although mixed bathing was usually available – if you knew the right place – it was generally frowned upon and houses would have either separate facilities for men and women or separate times.

Wherever their Empire spread, the Romans built baths. And when their empire fell, as if to shrug off every last vestige of the old imperial ways, Europeans lost interest in bathing altogether and stayed dirty for nearly 1500 years.

Modern Perfumes

The first modern perfume is thought to be Hungary Water, possibly invented by a hermit in 1370 and given to Elizabeth of Hungary, who suffered from crippling rheumatism. Bathing daily in clear spirit – in which lavender, rosemary and myrtle had macerated – apparently not only cured her rheumatism but also restored her beauty.

During the Italian Renaissance, Catherine de' Medici's own perfumier introduced his art to France. Near the Côte d'Azur, around Grasse – now the world centre of perfume production – the cultivation of flowers and aromatic plants has been a major industry since the eighteenth century, and jasmine, brought to France by the Moors in the sixteenth century, is a key ingredient.

The main impetus for developing and using perfume in Europe was the rank smell of the unwashed – rich and poor alike – and poor sanitation. Used in place of soap and water, perfume was applied to clothing, furniture, even accessories in a battle against not only malodorous smells but also disease; many herbs, such as lavender, do in fact have disinfectant properties.

Modern commercial processes now use distillieries to synthesise aroma compounds, allowing for perfumes that were once unattainable from aromatics alone. And the best are still, of course, fabulously expensive.

Left: A twentieth century advertisement for Cashmere Bouquet – the first milled perfumed soap – appeals to the market with an exotic subcontinental image.

The Secret of Milky White Skin

The milk of an ass is reputed to have almost miraculous cosmetic properties. Cleopatra, Queen of Egypt, according to legend, kept 700 asses so she could bathe in their milk every day. A female ass, or donkey, produces up to 300 ml (½ pint) of milk per day. Therefore 700 donkeys must have produced about 233 litres (51 gallons). The average modern bath holds 80 litres (17½ gallons) of water. This means either that Cleopatra's bath was an uneconomical three times larger than the modern version, or that she was bathing three times a day. Poppaea, the second wife of Nero, Emperor of Rome, with admirable restraint, made do with a mere 500 donkeys.

Top: An ancient Egyptian kohl tube in ivory.

Paint, Patches & the Perfect Smile

The quest for beauty was ever fraught with danger. Seekers have been burned, scalded and poisoned. They have been attacked by agonising illness, madness, debilitation, paralysis. They have been gored by bulls and eaten by crocodiles as they rummaged through their waste. Yet they held fast to the faith that one day they will be able to confront a mirror and utter the magic words: 'Looking good!'.

Right: Max Factor's Beauty Calibrator, invented in 1932, which enabled the makeup artist to compare a woman's facial measurements with the 'perfect' ideal and correct any discrepancies with makeup.

Far right: Applying mascara with an eyelash stencil, 1926. This method surely required much practice.

Above: Testing the wearability of lipstick by kissing a piece of glass, 1955. Presumably if the product smudged, it was back to the drawing board.

Croc Poo and Bull Bile

Makeup, or at least bodypaint, came before clothes. Before the advent of *Homo sapiens*, there's strong evidence to suggest that Neanderthals were brightening up their body hair with red ochre and may even have been making an extra effort with eyeliner and lipstick. Shells containing traces of pigment, which archaeologists reckon could have been part of a Neanderthal's makeup kit, have been found.

Certainly by the time the ancient Egyptians came along, makeup had become a sophisticated art, of which we have a fairly detailed knowledge, thanks to their habit of burying their dead with

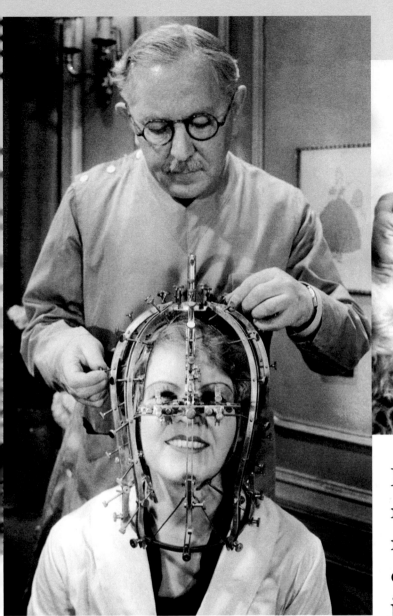

For their skincare regimen, Egyptians made a facemask from crocodile faeces and juniper leaves.

all the little luxuries and necessities of life. In ancient Egypyt makeup was unisex. Both men and women applied rouge and lip ointments and used henna to tint their fingernails.

The most striking feature of Egyptian maquillage was the eye makeup. First you line the lower lid with a green powder made from crushed malachite. Then comes the kohl – a paste of lead, antimony and magnesium oxide. Draw a thick line along the upper lid. Extend it towards the ear. Kohl has practical uses, too. It's a disinfectant and an insect repellant, and it helps protect the eyes from the sun's glare. When the eyes are appropriately feline and feral,

just trace the veins on your temples and chest with blue paint, tip your nipples with gold and you are good to go.

For their skincare regimen, Egyptians made a facemask from crocodile faeces and juniper leaves. If you were fresh out of croc poo, bullocks' bile or an ostrich egg were both acceptable substitutes.

The Flower Pout

In China makeup for women underwent only subtle changes over a period of 4000 years or so. The first step was to get that all-over chalky, blank look by shaving off the eyebrows and dusting the face with rice powder or crushed pearls. Next, reposition the eyebrows,

make them short and thick, then get to work on the mouth. Chinese lipstick was made of plant extracts, blood or crushed stone and from about 600 AD was available as a stick. Lip fashions changed over the years. During the Han Dynasty, a big red dot on the lower lip and a cupid's bow on the upper was the accepted look.

A thousand years later most women were painting a petal on the lower lip and two petals on the upper to make a small flower pout. There were many variations, making the imprint that a kiss would leave on a man's neck as individual as a signature – and a terrible telltale for the faithless.

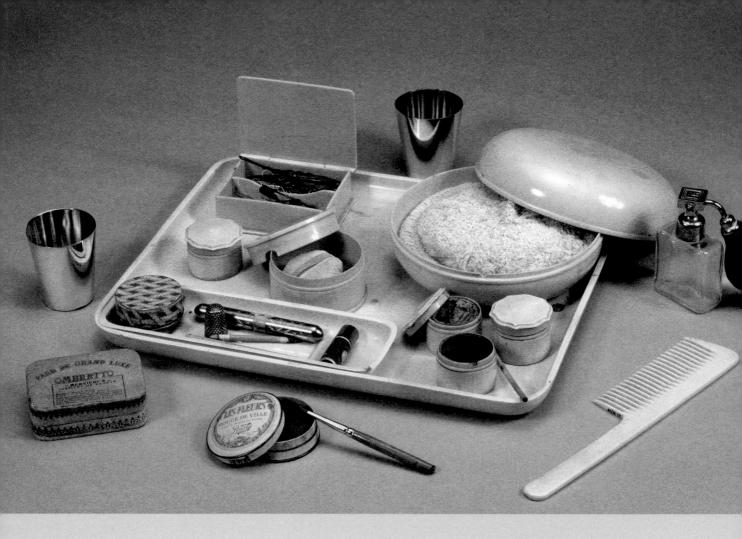

In the 1930s, Lash-Lure, a highly toxic eyelash dye, caused sixteen cases of blindness and one death bedore it was withdrawn from sale, and Koremlu, a depilatory cream, was found to contain quantities of rat poison.

The Maquillage of Death

The roll call of those who have given their lives to look fashionable, pretty or, in some cases, just vaguely presentable is tragically long.

The fashion of basting oneself from hairline to cleavage with a concoction mainly composed of white lead killed thousands, maybe millions. It barely abated from Roman times to the end of the eighteenth century, and was practised from the Imperial Palace in Beijing to the cold courts of northern Europe. In Japan it is thought to have brought premature death and disease to the elegant wives of the Samurai class and, most tragically of all, to the children who suckled lead at their mother's painted breasts.

When the lead began to scar, the pockmarks would customarily be filled with a mixture containing mercury – another killer. That's only if the user could actually see the pockmarks, after spending years squirting the appropriately named deadly nightshade into the eyes to achieve those attractive dilated pupils.

It wasn't as if people were ignorant of the cosmetics' lethal effects. In the seventeenth century an enterprising lady called Giulia Tofana marketed a face powder called the 'Manna of St Nicholas' to the ladies of Rome, which contained arsenic and lead. Signora Tofana instructed her patrons to be careful not to ingest any of the powder themselves but to always wear it when their husbands were around. After 600 husbands had died, the authorities launched an investigation. The powder was, of course, deadly. Giulia and some of her assistants were executed, but she maintained to the end that the wives knew exactly what they were doing.

A Victim of Cosmetics

Maria Gunning was a great Irish beauty who went to London and married into a title. Although naturally stunning, the Countess of Coventry became a slave to fashionable artifice and slathered her face with white-lead foundation and red-lead rouge. Her skin developed fissures, which became infected. In 1760, aged 27, she died of blood poisoning. The press described her as a 'victim of cosmetics'.

Before she died, according to Thomson Willing's *Old Time Beauties*, 'My lady lay on a couch, a pocket-glass constantly in hand, grieving at the gradual decay. The room was darkened, that others might not discern that which so chagrined her.'

As recently as the early twentieth century, products with names such as 'Laird's Bloom of Youth', 'Berry's Freckle Ointment' and 'Milk and Roses' all sold like hotcakes despite containing mercury, lead, carbolic acid or some other poison. In the 1930s, Lash-Lure, a highly toxic eyelash dye, caused sixteen cases of blindness and one death before it was withdrawn from sale, and Koremlu, a depilatory cream, was found to contain quantities of rat poison.

Apparently all were well worth trying, particularly if you were planning an open casket.

Opposite: An English makeup set, made principally of ivory, nineteenth century.

Above: A 1795 portrait of Maria Gunning. Her husband would not allow her to wear lead-based rouge on a trip to Paris; if only she had heeded his concerns.

Right: A poster for Rosée Crême, a 'pink cream' for the mouth and body, c.1895.

Polishing with Pumice Stone

Although the bright white smile has always been prized, outside China the toothbrush as we know it today was a long time coming.

In many parts of the world, the chew stick – a form of brush made, as the same suggests, by chewing a stick until it's sufficiently frayed – has been and, in some cases, still is, used. Often the wood is carefully chosen – the neem tree, favoured in India, has medicinal properties. Elsewhere the antiseptic arak tree is popular.

The Egyptians chewed natron and rinsed their mouths with a wash of goose fat, honey, frankincense and cumin. The Romans cleaned their teeth with a pumice stone, raising the possibility that the eruption of Vesuvius might have been seen as a tragedy for Pompeii but a great gift to tooth care.

In Japan they abandoned the battle for dental hygiene altogether and made black teeth a virtue, and the fashionable few whose teeth remained resolutely white would blacken them with a paint made from iron filings – a practice that didn't die out entirely until a law was passed in 1870.

For the most part, however, people tended to use toothpicks for the worst detritus but otherwise left their smiles to rot. The great breakthrough in Europe happened some time in the fifteenth century, when the first toothbrushes appeared, probably from China. Even then it was a good 200 years before tooth-brushing became a general habit, and another 200 before anybody even thought of flossing.

Right: A Chinese toothpick holder in ivory, c.1790. In Europe, during the same period, toothpicks could be luxury items, made from precious metals and jewels.

LADIES PERFUMED CALENDAR 1899.

HOYT'S GERMAN COLOGNE

The most fragrant and lasting of all perfumes.

MANUFACTURED BY E·W·HOYT & CO. LOWELL, MASS. U.S.A.

PRICE:
TRIAL SIZE 25 CTS
MEDIUM SIZE 50 CTS
LARGE BOTTLES $1.00

RUBIFOAM FOR THE TEETH A PERFECT LIQUID DENTIFRICE

PRICE 25 CTS

In Japan they abandoned the battle for dental hygiene altogether and made black teeth a virtue, and the fashionable few whose teeth remained resolutely white would blacken them...

Patching Things Up

From the mid-sixteenth century onwards, a custom grew up among the ultra-fashionable elites of Europe of covering up blemishes and scars left by the various poxes – small or otherwise – and related ravages with

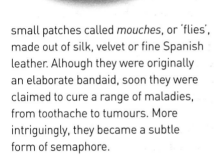

Right: This young woman, about to apply a *mouche*, seems to store her beauty spots in a large snuffbox.

Below: Madame du Barry was renowned for her delicate complexion.

small patches called *mouches*, or 'flies', made out of silk, velvet or fine Spanish leather. Alhough they were originally an elaborate bandaid, soon they were claimed to cure a range of maladies, from toothache to tumours. More intriguingly, they became a subtle form of semaphore.

Madame du Barry, the last mistress of Louis XV of France, supplied a key to the hidden meanings conveyed by the exact positioning of the *mouche*: near the upper lip – I want to kiss you; near the heart – I am feeling generous; and near the corner of the eye – I'm interested in you. On a big night out, particularly coquettish ladies often wore up to twelve *mouches*, no doubt plunging admirers into a fever of semiotic confusion.

And if that weren't complicated enough, in Britain the patches came to take on political meanings too. If you were a Whig sympathiser you exclusively patched your face on the right, while Tories kept to the left. It's hard to say what finally ended this bizarre craze – the discovery of the small pox vaccine, perhaps, or the opposition of the Church, or the realisation that, on balance, they did look very stupid.

In America, arsenic tablets were sold, and they were most effective in achieving that sought-after but terminal pale complexion.

le rouge baiser

calculé à paris par paul baudecroux

Opposite: An Ingres portrait of Princess de Broglie, a porcelain-skinned beauty who died of consumption in 1860 at 35.

Above: Highy desirable perfect skin in a detail from Ingres's *The Grand Odalisque*, 1814.

Left: *Le Rouge Baiser*, the first 'kiss-proof' lipstick, invented in 1927 by a French chemist.

Fainting in Coils

In Britain, during the Regency era, the fashionable outdoor look made rouge a big seller. Bushy eyebrows were prized, too. If yours didn't come up to scratch, false ones made from soft mouse hair could be stuck over the top. Powder puffs, face creams, perfume – both women and men jostled for a full range of beauty products and their place in front of the mirror. But a shadow of sobriety and modesty darkened the land as the nineteenth century wore on. Queen Victoria saw makeup as a vulgar affectation, fit only for actresses and prostitutes.

Where Regency gals were hearty, Victorian maids were delicate flowers, ideally beset by a terminal illness. Complexions were worn pale and translucent. To keep the skin safe from the punishing sun, parasols were carried outside and heavy velvet curtains drawn inside. Further blanching, it was thought, could come from drinking vinegar and chewing chalk. In America, arsenic tablets were sold, and they were most effective in achieving that sought-after but terminal pale complexion.

Most women practised their beauty routines in secret, far from the disapproving scowls of husband or father. In the kitchen they would mix face masks from oatmeal, honey and egg yolks, cleanse with rosewater or vinegar, massage castor oil into their eyelashes, buff their nails and, if they were feeling particularly devilish, use a little rice powder on that shiny nose.

Modern Times

With the Industrial Age came fancier powders, pomades and foundations in extravagantly named colours, but it was a while before that aura of Victorian disapproval could be shrugged off entirely. When Mrs Frances Hemmings opened her 'Household of Beauty' in London, ladies of quality would enter discreetly through a back door for their private consultations and walk out an hour or so later, laden with product that, if challenged, they would deny under oath ever using.

In America, a process called 'enamelling' gained popularity. It involved filling wrinkles and blemishes with a pliant paste then layering colours on top to produce the required dewy-fresh, even bloom. As long as the ladies didn't express too much emotion or dawdle near an open fire, the effect could last for up to a year.

The Hollywood star machine made the difference of course. It was clear from the start that the Egyptian lids and cupid pouts of the silent stars owed nothing to nature and everything to artifice. Boffins came up with cosmetic innovations such as 'flexible greasepaint' and 'colour harmony' face powder, which made sure the stars of stage and screen looked like stars, not ordinary people. When these, with the customary Hollywood spin, were released onto the marketplace, the marketplace was mobbed.

World War II finally severed that still-lingering link between cosmetics and bordello. In both North America and Britain it became every woman's patriotic duty to 'put her face on' and meet the world lipsticked, powdered rouged and resolute.

Blanket Coverage

The white lead face paints of the past had provided a thick, flexible cover and filler for blotches, blips, scars and zits. The trouble was they caused new blips. Big ones. And then they killed you. Not until the twentieth century were alternatives – concealers and camouflage makeup – devised that were just as effective as the old white lead but came with far, far less risk of a slow and painful death.

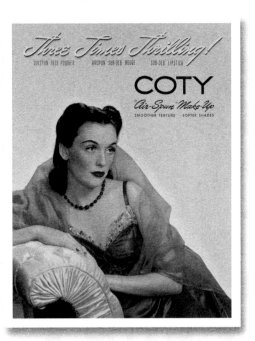

Left: English actress Dorothy Mackaill receives a lesson from the makeup master himself, Max Factor, 1930.

Right: A 1945 poster advertising the Coty 'Air-Spun' Make-Up range, which included powder, rouge and lipstick. The powder is still available.

Days of Port Wine and Rosacea

After college, Lydia O'Leary, born with a disfiguring 'port wine' birthmark on her face, worked first for a New York department store and then in a playing card factory. Messing with paints at the factory led her to experiment with various formulations for covering her birthmark. Some cracked as soon as they were dry, while others washed off as soon as they became wet.

Lydia joined forces with a chemist, eventually inventing a liquid preparation which, in 1932, she patented and marketed under the trade name 'Covermark' – 'The Modern Miracle' 'makes skin blemishes disappear from sight instantly'.

It was a ground-breaking moment in the history of makeup, and women around the world with less than perfect complexions rejoiced.

The Artistry of Makeup

Meanwhile, in Hollywood, Max Factor, who'd been providing makeup for movie actors since 1904, was bothered by a technological development. Technicolor demanded the reinvention of makeup. Shiny greasepaint, when it was filmed, reflected surrounding colours. Stars, suspicious of being seen with green and purple faces, boycotted the process. It took two years to develop a water-based product that left an opaque matte finish. Called Pan-Cake, it was first used in *Vogues of 1938*. When, in the same year, the new makeup was released to the general public, Pan-Cake sold like hot cake.

Heroes of Concealment

World War II left thousands with burns and scars. Military doctors knew that, when treating a case of facial burns, half the battle was psychological. If the scars could at least be effectively concealed, the patients might feel sufficiently confident to face the world.

Covermark and Pan-Cake were both pressed to the cause and served well, but on both sides of the Atlantic doctors sought still more effective formulations. In the United States, Elizabeth Arden did her bit for the war effort by producing a scar cream and touring hospitals to demonstrate its efficacy.

In the United Kingdom, Sir Archibald McIndoe of the British Association of Plastic Surgeons not only worked closely with Max Factor but also commissioned chemist Thomas Blake to develop a specialist product.

The result, 'Veil Cover Cream', was subjected to rigorous military testing by the Guinea Pig Club – a group of RAF casualties who had volunteered their injuries for experimental plastic surgery techniques and now had the courage to walk into their local pub slathered in often bright orange makeup. Adjustments were made, and the colours were adjusted.

It is thanks to the selfless efforts of these and other heroes that now, when the zit strikes or the thread vein spreads, there lurks in the makeup bag a little tube of magic guaranteed to match the skin tone and render all imperfection invisible.

Until the 1930s the average makeup kit was relatively simple. Suddenly, 'beauty' was worth millions.

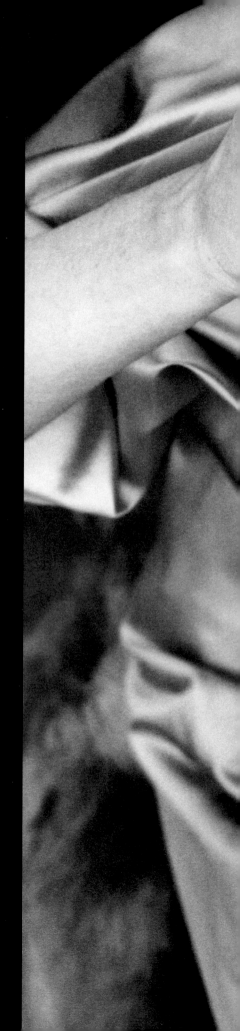

Above: In 1940 you might have worn a satin gown with fur cuffs as you gazed into a silver-backed hand mirror and perfected your indelible lipstick.

Right: In the same decade, you had to mix eyeliner with water before applying it with a brush – not a technique recommended for the novice.

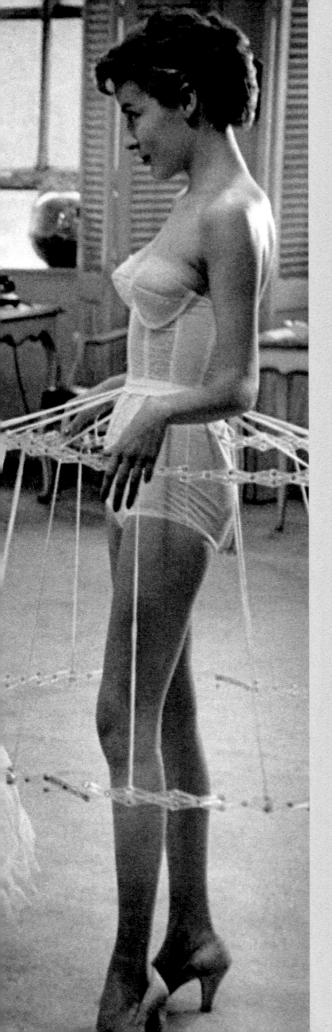

7
under-world

A woman in a corset is a lie, a falsehood, a fiction, but for us, this fiction is better than the reality. EUGENE CHAPUS, 1800–1877

Wasp Waists & Whalebone

One of woman's greatest battles down the ages – at times greater even than the struggle against injustice, oppression and the denial of opportunity – has been the struggle to draw breath. We look back to the days when beauty without cruelty was not an option, when the fashion victim was exactly that, when dressing to kill often rebounded. Until you had cracked ribs, spinal damage and a peculiarly positioned liver, you weren't really trying. This is the world of whalebone and steel, of leather and lacing – the world where elastic is for cowards.

Above: Caricature of a woman being photographed in her undergarments, 1901. Her corset sports a couple of suspenders for holding up her stockings.

Straight-Laced Ladies and Loose Women

Corsets are about class as well as aesthetics. Rich women sat (literally) straight-laced and were attended by servants. Trussed up and barely able to bend, they demonstrated that they were clearly *not* the sort of women who cut corn or pummelled laundry, or indeed were capable of getting dressed on their own. Lacing up a corset without a lady's maid to help requires great ingenuity. In contrast, the poor, if they were lucky enough to have any spare flesh, let it all hang out.

Early corseting was incorporated into the dress. The stomacher, a feature of many designs from the fifteenth to the eighteenth century, was a triangular piece of fabric, often stiffened or boned, and usually elaborately decorated, sewn into either the dress or underclothes (see page 54). It held in the belly and moulded the figure to the approximate 'required shape'. But sometimes achieving the 'required shape' called for something more extreme.

For a brief and glorious twenty years between about 1790 and 1810, skirts hung loose from the bosom down and the corset was abandoned. When it returned, it was as if women had to be punished for their years of freedom. Steel bars were commonplace. Mass production had democratised the corset. Cost was no longer an excuse for going corsetless, not that excuses were needed. Stout suburban ladies seemed only too keen to squeeze themselves into this former status symbol. To train them for adult life, even children were strapped into corsets. It was as if, for the whole of Queen Victoria's reign, the world – or at least the female half of the Western world – held its breath.

Rib-Crushing Machine

During the sixteenth century, Catherine de' Medici, Queen of France, liked to control. She imposed strict rules on her courtiers, dictating every aspect of their appearance, including, for the ladies, a 33-cm (13-in) waist. To achieve this impossible ideal, she designed a corset – a hip-to-shoulder steel framework. The wearer could tighten it a little more every day until the desired silhouette was achieved. And probably a few ribs were crushed.

Above: Catherine de' Medici (1519–1589).

Above left: A satirical look at corsetry, entitled 'A Correct View of Winding Up the Ladies', c.1830.

Left: A steel corset, decorated with pierced scrollwork, from the mid-seventeenth century. Of course it may have been used for remedial purposes.

The Empress of Thin

The Empress Elisabeth of Austria (1837–1898), known to her friends as Sisi, was a highly educated scholar, a brilliant linguist, a competition-standard equestrian and a much respected and liberal-minded monarch. Her beauty and fine figure were spoken of in breathless tones throughout the courts of Europe.

She passed on her fear of body mass to her children. It is reported that when her youngest daughter first met the delightfully dumpy Queen Victoria of England, the poor child was terrified.

The 'wasp waist' was in fashion. At a reputed 41 cm (16 in), Sisi's waist was heading away from wasp towards ant. Her figure was maintained by an unhealthy relationship with food that accurately foreshadowed the lifestyles of celebrities a hundred years later. She also took a great deal of exercise –

Above: 'I spy four sizes just like the women in my life – Fifine, my favourite, that great whore Cocotte, tall Mimi and my wife up there in the corner.'

Left: Elisabeth of Austria (1837–1898) indulged in some strange beauty rituals. One, to keep her waist slim, was to sleep with cloths soaked in cider on her hips.

Above: In 1873, Dr Lucien Warner, a prominent New York physician who was concerned about the effect of the corset on women's health, designed the Coraline Health Corset, made from two pieces of fabric – obtained from *Agave americana* – laced or fastened together.

riding, fencing and working out in the gym she had built at the palace. But her real secret was the corset.

Most of Sisi's contemporaries favoured an almost forgiving corset, which fastened at the front with hooks and eyes. To achieve the compression that her uncompromising standards demanded, Sisi ordered laced corsets from Paris. And to be sure they would stand up to the strains she had in mind, she had them made of leather. The lacing procedure would take anything up to an hour. She was sewn into her clothes, and wore no underwear other than her corset for fear that even the finest silk would add ugly bulk. To this day she remains, of course, an icon in the fetish world.

In 1898 Sisi took a holiday to Lake Geneva in Switzerland. While hurrying to catch a steamer, she was approached by Luigi Lucheni, an Italian anarchist. He struck her, appearing to punch her chest, but his fist concealed a long and lethal blade. Although the dagger entered Sisi's heart, she was able to carry on walking for a hundred metres or more, and even then it was some time before she died. At the autopsy, the coroner discovered the reason for her resilience – her tight-laced corset had acted like a tourniquet, restricting internal as well as external bleeding.

Right: A nineteenth-century shop display for a corset, which fastened at the front with hooks and eyes.

English writer Aldous Huxley described the Edwardian
woman as 'a crab shelled in whalebone'.

'A Crab Shelled in Whalebone'

The fashionable female silhouette
changed completely in the late
nineteenth and early twentieth
centuries due to a new style of corset
worn underneath the clothes. English
writer Aldous Huxley described the
Edwardian woman as 'a crab shelled
in whalebone' but, although the chic
ladies of that era were restricted by
their corsets, they were less likely to
sustain permanent damage than the
'tight-lacers' of the nineteenth century.

In fact, the Edwardian shape first
emerged as a response to medical
evidence on the dangers posed to
women's health by the wasp waist.
In the 1890s, the Parisian corsetière
Inès Gâches-Sarraute, who had studied
medicine, designed a new 'reform
corset' with a straight-fronted busk,
which supported the abdomen and
left the thorax free, and suspenders,
which replaced garters. It also gave
the wearer a forward-tilted posture
that showed off a fine décolletage.

Meanwhile, in the late nineteenth
century, various advocates of dress
reform emerged, the most famous
of these being Amelia Bloomer. The
reformers generally recommended
less restrictive undergarments,
although few went as far as advocating
that women should abandon corsets
altogether. A minority of artistically
minded ladies wore the 'Aesthetic'
fashions, softly draping clothes
influenced by historical costume, with
no corsets, but they were considered
eccentric by the majority of women.

Right: The straight-fronted corset, according to a 1901
article in *The Lady's Magazine*, 'is likely to create a new
style of waist and figure entirely'. It was the 'S' curve
(see page 39).

The Long-line Corset

In about 1907, fashions changed yet again, and the look became long and svelte, sometimes tubular, as in the 'hobble' skirt (see page 41). Corsets thus became very long and straight, reaching down to the upper thigh. This very long-line corset (sometimes as long as 45 cm (18 in) from the waist down) could be very uncomfortable, as it not only confined the legs and rubbed badly but also made it impossible to sit down. However, corset technology was developing, substituting elastic for boning, and allowing greater flexibility.

The War Years and the Exotic

The war years, 1914–18, brought in looser, more comfortable, shapeless clothes. The exotic, vividly coloured costumes of the *Ballets Russes* were a huge influence, as were the seductive dances of Nijinsky and Karsavina. Women, longing for more freedom, were also becoming active in sport. A new generation of corsetry was emerging, and the separate brassière and girdle were beginning to be worn by more daring and modern women.

In this medical illustration from about 1880 (right), we can see how a woman's tight-laced corset not only over-inflated her lungs but also made her diaphragm push down her internal organs. The corset restricted her breathing and could even suppress her appetite.

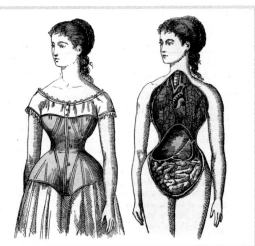

Above: Lacing a portly Regency gentleman into his corset required the assistance of a valet and no small amount of brute force.

The Fatness of King George

At his coronation in 1821, George IV of England fell ill. He came close to passing out. Public pronouncements blamed the heat and the great weight of his coronation robes, but everybody knew it was his corset. By the end of his life, George IV's waistline had spread to 140 cm (55 in) but, cinched into a corset, he could get it down to 127 (50).

'Body Belts'

Men took up corsets towards the end of the eighteenth century, just about the time that women temporarily abandoned them. In was the broad-shouldered, narrow-waisted athletic look, as were tighter clothes that left no room for ambiguity. You either had it or you didn't. Sometimes they called their corsets 'body belts'. Sometimes they pretended they were wearing them for 'medical reasons', such as back pain. No one was fooled for a moment.

The Liberty Bodice

In 1908, Fred Cox, Marketing Director at R.W. and H. Symington & Co. of Market Harborough, England, invented the Liberty Bodice (known in the United States as the Emancipation Bodice). It was a response to years of stern warnings about the perils of corsetry.

For years doctors had been claiming, not without justification, that tight-lacing caused red noses, liver failure, headaches, dizziness, constipation, hysteria, indigestion and no end of damage to the 'plaguy vessels' of the abdomen. The corset manufacturers responded by extolling the 'healthy' properties of their products. Rubber was incorporated to hold in the flesh 'more naturally', and meshing to allow the flesh to 'breathe'.

Brave pioneers began to throw away their corsets. Healthy, active Americans of both sexes started wearing the much more comfortable 'Liberty Suit' or 'combinations', which were devoid of stiffening or bones (see page 184).

The anti-corset murmurs grew louder when the Lady Cyclists Association and the Rational Dress Society denounced any clothing 'that either deforms the figure, impedes the movements of the body, or in any way tends to injure the health'.

The Liberty Bodice was the answer to a Lady Cyclist's Prayer. Originally designed for children, the bodice was a sort of waistcoat, made of fleecy wool, which fastened at the front with rubber buttons. Some versions had tapes and fittings, allowing it to be attached to stockings and other underwear. Although it had no compression properties, the fabric was substantial enough to smooth the worst lumps, bumps and creases.

From its provenance as a healthy alternative to the corset, the Liberty Bodice developed a totemic reputation as a bringer of health, both physical and moral, and it became immensely popular for girls, boys and women.

Right up until the 1960s, American grandmothers were still certain that going out without a Liberty Bodice – even in the height of summer – would be an open invitation to colds, flu, polio and cholera.

JFK –
The Truth

John Fitzgerald Kennedy, the thirty-fifth President of the United States, had suffered back problems since early childhood. Throughout his presidency, he wore a tight corset of canvas and steel. Kennedy was wearing it as he sat waving from the back of the Lincoln Continental as it drove slowly down Dealey Plaza, Dallas on 22 November 1963. When the first bullet struck him in the neck, some extreme physical reaction – to cower, to collapse – would have been natural. But tragically Kennedy, corseted, could move only his head. He remained upright and immobile – a perfect target for the second, fatal bullet.

Right: The French actress Polaire (1879–1939), whose waist measurement is alarmingly waspish.

Below: This early version of the brassière is more like a camisole than the modern bra (see page 180).

Right: In the early 1950s you could dispense with the girdle and go for a suspender belt. This one matches the V-shaped bra.

Far right: A black bra and matching girdle with a control panel, 1952. It may have taken you some time to wrestle yourself into it.

Below: A 1946 advertisement for a bra and girdle, from *Femina* magazine.

Scandale

GAINES
CEINTURES·
SOUTIEN-GORGE

A-Bra-Cad-A-Bra

The Minoans of Crete knew about the push-up. In India they had the *kanchuka* to lift and separate, and in China the *dudou*. In ancient Greece they wore the *apodesmos,* and in Roma the *mamillare*. Its various functions have been to cover, reduce, restrain, enhance or support the breasts. We call it a brassière – literally, 'little camisole'.

Although it was common for women in ancient Egypt and other cultures to go bare-breasted, the practical advantages of some sort of support must have always been apparent. Greek women who preferred to expose their breasts would often either tie the *apodesmos* below the breasts, to give support, or wear a simple belt called a *strophion* in the same way.

Burning Rubber

In 1874, Elizabeth Stuart Phelps – feminist, spiritualist and vehement advocate of dress reform – advised women to burn their corsets. As far as we know, no one at the time followed Ms Phelps's advice, but the relationship between feminism and the burning of restrictive underwear seems to have remained in the public consciousness. Certainly when the Women's Liberation Movement began to demonstrate in the late 1960s, the participants felt the need to burn something. At a 1968 demonstration in Atlantic City, New Jersey, a bra was placed in a garbage can along with other symbols of oppression. Although the idea of torching the lot was mooted, the appropriate permits could not be obtained. A couple of years later, in Berkeley, California, a 38C was burned with appropriate fire-prevention equipment at the ready.

From about the fourteenth century, the functions of the bra were addressed by either stiffening in the dress or the corset, which could push up, push out, flatten or otherwise flatter, according to the current dictates of style.

There is no 'inventor' of the modern bra. The London Science Museum has a very early cleavage-enhancing bra, designer unknown, dating from the early years of the nineteenth century. In 1859, Henry Lesher of New York patented a 'corset substitute' that could provide 'symmetrical rotundity', and in the ensuing years variations on the basic theme came and went. A design catering for the large-breasted woman was awarded a bronze medal by the Massachusetts Charitable Mechanics Association. Lingeriste Herminie

Above: The American actress Jayne Mansfield wears a knit top over her pointy bra, which formed the bust into the desirable pointy shape of the 1950s.

By the 1890s the word 'brassière' was cropping up in women's magazines, and in 1911 it made its first appearance in the Oxford English Dictionary.

Cadolle's *Le Bien-Être,* or Well-Being, which supported the breasts from above with shoulder straps, rather than from below with whalebone, was a hit at the Paris *Exposition Universelle.*

By the 1890s the word 'brassière' was cropping up in women's magazines, and in 1911 it made its first appearance in the *Oxford English Dictionary.*

Businessman, aviator and engineer, Howard Hughes used his engineering nouse to solve the problem of holding up Jane Russell's ample bosom in the 1943 movie *The Outlaw.* He constructed a special cantilevered 'push-up' bra, which contained various steel structures more usually called for in the building of bridges. The resulting bra was certainly push-up but it was also unfortunately very uncomfortable.

By the mid-1960s the ideal waist to hip ratio was considered to be 61 to 86 cm (24 to 34 in). A girdle could whip off a critical couple of centimetres.

Opposite: A bra with a satin and net girdle, 1938.

Above: A strapless black corselet or basque with suspenders sits over a white petticoat, a critical undergarment for skirt shapes in the 1950s. (For more on petticoats, see pages 18, 22, 26 and 32.)

Right: A high-waisted girdle with a V-shaped control panel and suspenders, 1953.

Codpieces & Bloomers

Adam and Eve's use of fig leaves began the fashion — prevalent pretty much ever since — of keeping the private parts private. Essentially all that's required is some simple winding or binding, but fashion was ever a stranger to the simple and a scorner of the obvious.

Above: A hand-coloured fashion plate for pantaloons and a dress, from the famous French magazine, *Le Follet Courrier des Salons*, 1834.

A Gap in the Market

As men's tunics became shorter in the late Middle Ages, a gap in the market was revealed. Men's hose consisted of two separate legs laced together at the top in a way that left the parts that should be private glaringly public.

The codpiece began as a modest triangular piece of fabric ('cod' being the contemporary slang for male genitalia). It was fashion leaders such as Henry VIII of England who appreciated the unique opportunity presented by the codpiece. Following the boastful king's example, codpieces were puffed out, padded, shaped and even bejewelled.

Codpieces shrank beneath the icy gaze of Henry's daughter, Elizabeth I. Under her influence court fashion for men became more feminised, more streamlined – sleeves became less puffy and doublets lost their outrageous padding. By the end of her reign the codpiece, in its inflated form, had all but disappeared.

The Boxer Rebellion

After the demise of the codpiece, men generally wore demure drawers of cotton or linen. The invention of the spinning jenny in 1764 made cotton more widely available, and factories began to mass-produce underwear.

Patented in 1868, the 'Union Suit' was sold in stores all over the United States, then came to England – renamed 'Combinations' – and thence the world. Traditionally made from red flannel, the one-piece garment had long sleeves and legs, buttons from crotch to neck and a flap in the rear, called a drop seat, also held in place with buttons. In rural areas it was often donned in autumn and not removed until spring.

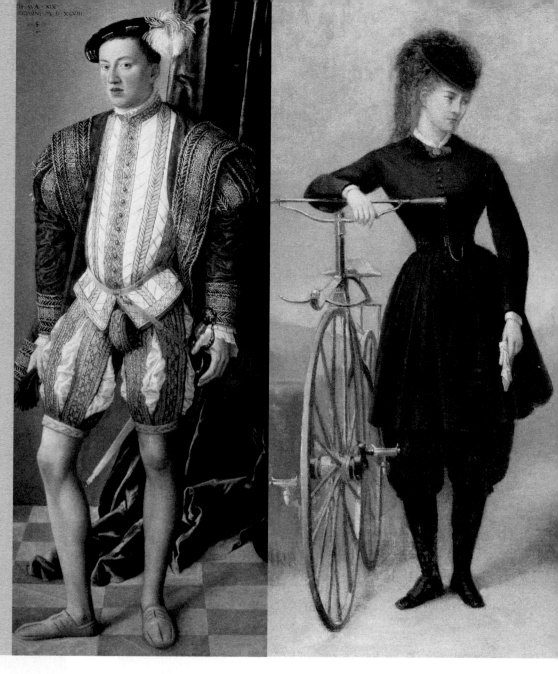

The history of twentieth century underwear is largely the history of lingeristes charging more and more for less and less.

Right: Archduke Ferdinand of Tyrol wears a codpiece with slashed sleeves and doublet, 1548.

Far right: Blanche d'Antigny, the French actress who was also Émile Zola's model for the courtesan in his novel *Nana*, sensibly dressed for riding a velocipede.

In about 1920, the union suit split into two and men started to wear undergarments based on the shorts worn by professional boxers, without buttons and flaps but with a convenient elasticated waistband.

In the 1930s, an 'apparel engineer' named Arthur Kneibler came up with the briefest of briefs, which featured a Y-shaped front opening, introducing for the first time the Y-front.

Pantalettes and Bloomers

Until the eighteenth century, women didn't bother much with underwear. It was considered unhealthy. Catherine de' Medici, Queen of France, had pioneered the wearing of long pants under her skirts when out riding, but it wasn't until after the French Revolution that the fashion for flimsy, diaphanous dresses created a demand for a good stout pair of drawers.

Pantalettes originally comprised two separate garments, one for each leg (which is why we still say a pair of knickers or pants), tied around the waist and leaving the crotch open. These expanded to become pantaloons, the voluminous waist-to-ankle underwear worn to prevent an accidental crinoline tilt exposing bare leg.

A baggier version of pantaloons – designed as outerwear and named 'bloomers' in honour of their staunchest advocate Amelia Bloomer – were briefly fashionable in the 1850s, but remained in the public consciousness so that when something similar re-emerged in the 1900s as underwear, they too were called 'bloomers'. Time passed. They shrank. The history of twentieth century underwear is largely the history of lingeristes charging more and more for less and less.

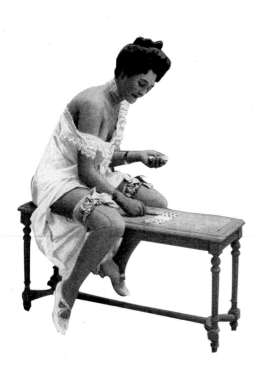

Stockings & Nylons

Socks for warmth, stockings for beauty. Humankind waited a long time for the invention of properly functioning, affordable stockings. While men in tights spent several centuries wrestling with wrinkles, bagging and inefficient gartering, women of the northern latitudes sensibly put their legs away for two millennia, and did not get them out again until all these difficulties had been properly ironed out.

Left: An embroidered men's silk stocking, England, c.1720.

Far left: A 'naughty' postcard from the early twentieth century of a woman playing cards in a slip, her stockings secured with garters.

Calves and Garters

In 1509, at the marriage of Henry VIII of England to Catherine of Aragon, one of the Spanish court's gifts to the king was a pair of knitted silk stockings. Such thin and form-fitting elasticity had not been seen before in England. Henry, an athlete who was particularly proud of his well-muscled calves, loved them. To avoid wrinkles he kept them gartered so tight that, when ulcers appeared on his legs, lack of blood circulation prevented their healing. The ulcers plagued him for the rest of his life.

It seems that for the next fifty years, Spain was the only source of these top-of-the-range tights. They were probably made by Spanish Moors, Muslims who had brought the art of fine knitting from the East and the

William Lee, an English inventor, loved a woman. But the woman loved knitting. Jealous, and somewhat driven to distraction by the constant clack of her needles, he set himself the task of devising a machine that could dispense with hand-knitting altogether, leaving women free to devote themselves to their menfolk.

Lee built his first Stocking Frame Knitting Machine in 1589, and spent the rest of his life improving it. Eventually, with twenty needles, it could knit silk to a Spanish standard. Queen Elizabeth was not impressed and refused him a patent, ostensibly because of the perceived threat to the hand-knitting industry but more likely because she feared that mass production would put the tights of queens within the reach of any Tom, Dick or Harry.

When Lee's business partner, entirely coincidentally, was arrested for treason and executed, William had had enough. He fled to France, taking his machines with him, and established a thriving factory in Rouen, turning out silk and woollen stockings. Later his brother set up similar factories in England, in London and Nottingham. As Elizabeth had feared, within a generation the riff-raff were prancing in fancy tights.

Spanish Tights

Fancy tights were menswear. Women, wearing floor-length skirts, wore hose for warmth and comfort, not beauty. Nevertheless, Queen Elizabeth was delighted by a gift of Spanish tights, in black, from Mary Montague, her Lady of the Bedchamber – doubly pleasing because Elizabeth knew that her cousin and rival, Mary Stuart of Scotland, had been swanning around in Spanish tights for several years.

Middle East. They were a rich man's luxury. Henry II of France wore a pair to his sister's wedding. August, the Elector of Saxony, owned eight pairs.

Billy Lee's Magic Machine

By the middle of the sixteenth century, most European countries had developed a cottage industry in hand-knitting, although none could produce work as fine as that made in Spain.

Fancy tights were menswear. Women, wearing floor-length skirts, wore hose for warmth and comfort, not beauty.

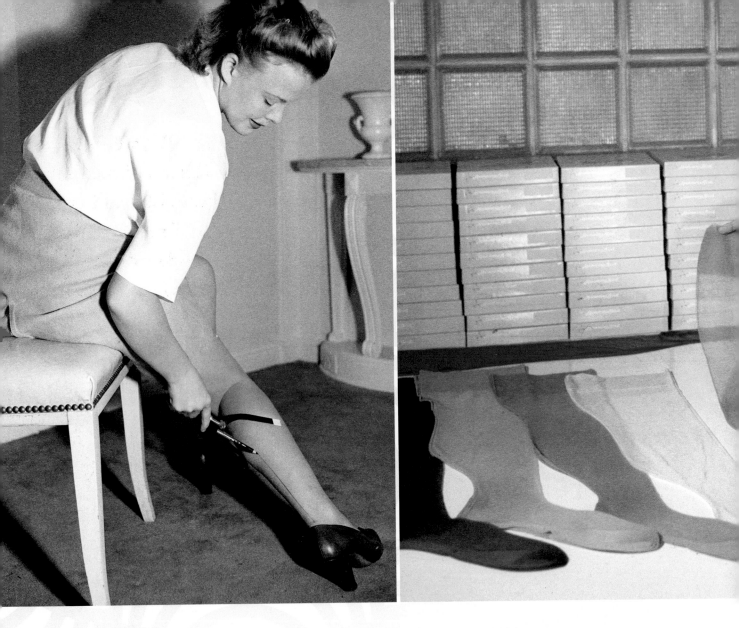

Socks

Socks are old. The first mention, possibly 3000 years ago – laying down some strict instructions that government ministers were not to appear in the presence of the emperor without first removing their shoes and socks – was recorded during the Chinese Zhou Dynasty.

The oldest pair of socks ever found is also Chinese. They're made of lined silk, and still good for wearing some 2000 years after being buried with Quanhou Licang, a prime minister.

On the other side of the Sea of Japan, the Japanese had also become sock lovers. The seal of approval was given when, in the sixteenth century, the elite Samurai warriors abandoned their bearskin boots and wore flip-flops – called 'thongs' in some parts of the world and 'jandals', or Japanese sandals, in others – instead. With disdain for fashion, in cold weather they wore these with white socks, called *tabi*, sewn from linen, and customised with a split toe for use with a flip-flop. These days *tabi* are likely to be made of stretch polyester, and remain an essential item of formal wear in Japan, obligatory for tea ceremonies, funerals and Ninja.

China, however, has never lost its pre-eminence in the world of socks. Datang, known as 'Sock Town', in Zhejiang Province, currently turns out eight billion pairs a year.

Sheer Genius

In the 1920s, as skirts became shorter, the need for a good-looking, non-baggy, affordable stocking became urgent. For a while black woollen stockings were ubiquitous, sometimes brightened up by embroidered patterns on the calves and knees, but by the early 1920s every bright young thing with bobbed hair and whirling pearls dreamed of silk – soft, sheer and utterly unaffordable.

Early disastrous experiments to manufacture an artificial silk eventually bore fruit with a version that did not burst into flames at inopportune moments. Given the name 'Rayon', it was a passable imitation of the real thing, but where silk had lustre, rayon

Given the name 'Rayon', it was a passable imitation of the real thing, but where silk had lustre, rayon shone. Enterprising flappers powdered their stockings to mitigate the glare.

shone. Enterprising flappers powdered their stockings to mitigate the glare.

In 1924, Wallace Carothers, Professor of Chemistry at Harvard University, began to research the chemical structure of polymers. After ten years he and his team had developed a new, improved 'artificial silk', called Nylon, initially used for fishing line and surgical sutures.

The first pair of nylon stockings was demonstrated at the 1939 New York World Fair; by the 1950s, 'nylons' was the new word for 'stockings'. But once pantyhose, which combined panties with stockings, became affordable in the late 1960s, stockings suddenly became associated with lingerie.

Above left: During World War II, when stockings were in short supply, Hollywood starlet Kay Bensel draws a seam line on the back of her leg with the aid of an eyebrow pencil, a screwdriver handle and a bicycle clip.

Above: Checking for snags and runs against a white table in a stocking factory in Chattanooga, Tennessee, 1948.

Right: An advertisement for luxury stockings and underwear from *Femina* magazine, 1949.

At the Beach

Swimwear is a newcomer to the world of fashion. There are illustrations of Roman maidens wearing fetching leather two-pieces but this was just for working out – skinny-dipping was the norm in rivers and lakes. The naked form, however, was never commensurate with style. 'What's the point of swimming,' the fashionable would cry, 'if it doesn't come with an outfit?'

Afraid to Come out of the Water

The idea that sea-bathing could be a pleasurable, healthy pursuit rather than the last resort of a luckless sailor first began to emerge in the eighteenth century. From the outset, at least for the wealthy and fashionable, the preservation of modesty took priority over any enjoyment. Bathing machines – small cabins on wheels in which the bathers could change before being trundled into the water – ensured that nobody had to parade on the beach in their swimsuits. The suits themselves were made of stiff canvas. It was vital, after all, that the fabric wouldn't cling when wet.

Things loosened up when the first railways began to fill beaches with the less well-off. Out went the bathing machines and the stiff canvas; in came figure-hugging woollen swimsuits for men, with long sleeves and legs, clearly based on the combination underwear that was popular at the time. Women swam in a two-piece affair, with a flannel gown from shoulder to knee and ballooning pantaloons down to the ankle. Corset manufacturers made special rustproof models, suitable for immersion.

It is a tribute to the strength and endurance of those Victorian swimmers that so few succumbed to the paralysing grip of the whalebone and the lethal drag of waterlogged flannel.

At the beginning of the twentieth century there emerged a woman who would sweep away these comic bathing

Above left: This 1900 cartoon anticipates the figure-hugging swimsuit, a legacy of Annette Kellerman's fight to swim unencumbered.

Above: In 1825, if you were to go bathing at Brighton's beach, in England, you'd have to change into your 'bathing dress' and slip discreetly into the sea from your bathing machine.

Right: Seventy-five years later, men had advanced to the all-in-one woollen swimsuit but women were still fully dressed, right down to their toes.

costumes forever – Annette Kellerman, an antipodean beauty who, at 18, had been the first woman to attempt to swim the English Channel. Kellerman's beauty was officially corroborated by professors at Harvard University who declared that her vital statistics were identical to those of the ancient Greek statue, the Venus de Milo.

In 1907, Annette, wearing a fetching skin-tight one-piece that ended just above her knees, was arrested on Revere Beach in Massachusetts for indecent exposure. At her trial she robustly asserted that in conventional bathing attire 'she may as well be swimming in chains' and the judge, impressed by her logic and classical credentials, dismissed the case.

Following Annette's brave example, swimwear began to shrink. Necklines migrated from the throat to the top of the bosom, legs were revealed up to the mid-thigh and sleeves disappeared altogether. Skirts vanished and the androgynous bathing beauties of the 1920s emerged from the waters wearing figure-hugging, wool jersey tank suits.

Within five years 'bikini' had become, like Hoover and Thermos, not only the brand but also the product itself, and any link with South Pacific atolls or nuclear tests had long been forgotten.

Above left: A blast at Bikini Atoll, July 1946.

Above: On Palm Beach, Florida, Betty Fringle has her bathing suit measured to ensure it conforms with censors' regulations, 1925.

Below left: In the 1960s bathing caps kept the fashionable stiff helmet of hair dry and intact.

Itsy Bitsy...

In 1946, the United States government relocated the reluctant population, along with their goats, of a small group of islands in the South Pacific. Over the next twelve years, they used the islands as a test site for twenty-three nuclear devices. This was the Bikini Atoll.

The radiation that resulted from these tests would blight the lives of the inhabitants of neighbouring islands for years to come, but at the time it all looked unbelievably exciting. Atomic meant a bright and wonderful future. Nuclear meant ba-doom!

Meanwhile, in Paris, Jacques Heim, a couturier and furrier, had designed a tiny two-piece bathing suit that he called the Atome after the smallest particle then known. To publicise it, he hired planes to skywrite: 'Atome – the world's smallest bathing suit'.

Three weeks later, Louis Réard, a French automobile engineer and heavily bespectacled amateur swimsuit designer, produced a two-piece of his own, called it the Bikini – believing that its impact would approximate that of a nuclear bomb – and hired planes to skywrite, 'Bikini – smaller than the

world's smallest bathing suit'. It was made from a mere 78 cm (30 in) of fabric. There was nothing new about the two-piece bathing costume. Victorian ladies had, after all, worn two-pieces – voluminous ones – and designer Carl Jantzen had come up with a sort of T-shirt and shorts version back in 1913.

But the bikini was the two-piece that everyone remembers. Within five years 'bikini' had become, like Hoover and Thermos, not only the brand but also the product itself, and any link with South Pacific atolls or nuclear tests had long been forgotten.

Above left: French actress Barbara Laage follows the latest fashion in a two-piece that she made herself from just 1 m (3 ft) of fabric, 1946.

Above: By 1958 girls could lounge around on the French Riviera, wearing bikinis, sipping rosé and smoking cigarettes, confident their swimwear would not be measured by the beach inspector.

Publicity Splash

Louis Réard, a consummate showman, told reporters that the only woman in Paris brave enough to wear his new creation was an exotic dancer from the Casino de Paris. Micheline Bernardini posed in Réard's 78 cm (30 in) of fabric at a municipal swimming pool in Paris, brandishing a matchbox into which the skimpy garment was supposed to fit while overhead more skywriters spelt the word BIKINI in 12 m (40 ft) high letters.

After Dark

Ah, the nightly dilemma – whether 'tis nobler to wear pyjamas, nightdress, negligée and peignor, underwear or nothing at all to sleep? For those who treat fashion as a 24/7 preoccupation, dressing for bed is as painstaking a business as dressing for the opera, where glamour and style always outweigh comfort and warmth.

Above: This spotted lawn nightgown, decorated with lace and roses, owes something to Edwardian day wear, 1914.

Above right: A mauve nightgown and dance slippers – the perfect outfit for an evening of seduction, 1955.

The Rise and Fall of the Gentleman's Nightie

Before the seventeenth century, only the highest in the land bothered much with sleepwear. Most people slept in a chemise, the universal undershirt worn by all but the poorest. Or if it was cold, they might remove their boots.

But the eighteenth century gent took as much care with his nightwear as his daywear. He went to bed awash in ruffs and cuffs and lace, teamed with either the classic pom-pommed nightcap or a loose linen turban (see page 127). If in mourning, everything would be black. Upon rising, he might put on a gorgeous banyan or *robe de chambre* – a huge kimono cut from metres of vivid silk – and top it with another turban in a contrasting shade.

Although the lace and frills disappeared, the fashion for a properly cut nightshirt, sometimes with neck and cuffs starched just like a dayshirt, persisted well into the nineteenth century. But with the dawn of the twentieth century came a new fashion

Negligent Lingering

A Victorian lady's nightdress was, give or take the odd scrap of ribbon, lace or broderie anglaise, pretty much identical to that of her husband. Its angelic whiteness, contour-concealing volume and high neckline – sometimes even featuring a chin-tickling ruff – broadcast unambiguous signals of purity and modesty. Some women wore their corsets in bed, perhaps hoping their flesh would set in the mould like a jelly. Similarly in France, women's nightwear, although already graced with the name negligée, was built for warmth but never seduction.

The first great change came in the 1920s, when a fashionable nightdress, made in coloured silk, rayon and taffeta, was indistinguishable from a fashionable evening dress. Worn with a peignoir in a matching fabric, it made a jolly ensemble in which to entertain a few late evening – or early morning – pals.

In the 1940s it became customary, to boost the troops' morale, for film stars to be photographed in their nightwear. Lacy, gauzy, low-cut and clinging were qualities much admired by the fighting forces. But already the gap between glamour and reality was yawning. A 1996 survey revealed that, unmoved by fashion plates or Valentine's gifts, most women sleep in stout but comfortable pyjamas.

that consigned the nightshirt, along with the farthingale and the periwig, to the dustbin of history.

In 1897 the *Tailor and Cutter* magazine was sad to announce: 'The doom of the nightshirt is written'. Their despair was brought on by the growing popularity of a new trend in sleepwear. Missionaries, soldiers and traders in India adopted the habit of sleeping in a loose-fitting suit of jacket and trousers, made of wool, silk or soft flannelette cotton, and known by its Hindi name, *pajama*.

Below: The demure cotton nightgown in this 1897 photograph is contradicted somewhat by the young woman's bare legs – Victorian erotica perhaps?

The word *peignoir*
is from the French
peigner, to comb, as
women used to wear
a robe while they
brushed their hair.

Above: Possibly a descendant of the bed jacket, short
and sheer babydoll pyjamas were popular in the 1960s.
They are still to be found in adult lingerie shops.

Right: In this still from a silent film, the actress wears
an extraordinary lace gown with fringes of beading.

Opposite: Preparing for bed in satin pyjamas and
pumps, as one does, is the actress Thalia Barbarova, in
1925. A sumptuous brocade shawl drips over her chair.

8
big wigs
to beehives

Three things are men
most likely to be cheated
in, a horse, a wig,
and a wife. BENJAMIN FRANKLIN, 1706–1790

Big Wigs

Wearing a wig has always been a practical solution for those who prefer to improve on their own inadequate locks or, indeed, need to conceal its absence. But throughout history there have been periods when excessively large wigs were highly fashionable. Welcome to the bizarre world of the big wig.

The Egyptian 'Bob'

The ancient Egyptians were responsible for the longest period of continuous wig-wearing. Both wall paintings and surviving artefacts show that everyone in the middle or upper classes, man or woman, wore a wig every day. The only wigless people were labourers and the very poor, who couldn't afford them; slaves, who were not entitled to wear them and priests, who always kept their heads shaved.

This custom continued throughout the Old, Middle and New Kingdoms, from about 3000 BC until about 300 AD. Interestingly, the Egyptians devised very few major changes in clothing fashions during all this time, keeping to well-established variations on the theme of white pleated linen. But throughout this period it was vital for a respectable ancient Egyptian to be seen dressed and wigged in the accepted style, their body hair removed.

Egyptian wigs – made of human hair or a mix of hair, plant fibres and wool attached to a palm-fibre base with resin or beeswax – were formed into a permanent style using more waxes. Many wigs were made of innumerable very fine braids; a popular style for noblewomen had three sections of braids, with two hanging on either side of the face and one down the back. For men, the usual style was shorter but wide, resulting in the characteristic 'heavy bob' that can be seen in so many Egyptian wall paintings.

Above left: Such was the apparent absurdity of women's hair in the late eighteenth century that cartoonists had fun satirising them.

Left: A painted ivory plaque showing Tutankhamun and his wife in a garden, both wearing stiff plaited wigs. The pharaoh's is the 'heavy bob' for men.

These wigs were valuable, so they were kept in wig boxes and scented with dried flowers and cinnamon. When an Egyptian person died, their wigs accompanied them to the afterlife.

The usual explanation for the Egyptian wig-wearing tradition was that it was easier to keep the head clipped or shaved for easy washing, then add the wig to protect the head from the weather. Natural hair would need to be thick to protect its wearer from the scorching Egyptian sun and the cold winter nights; it would also have been difficult to keep hair clean with the available shampooing materials. However, it's possible that, as with so many other trends over the centuries, it just came into fashion and lingered.

Chinese and Japanese Wigs

Wigs are mainly a Western affectation and, historically, have been used little in Asia, except for traditional theatre and entertainment. In China, however, it was customary in the Middle Ages for the empress to wear a ceremonial wig decorated with birds and flowers.

Above: A selection of Japanese wigs used in Kabuki theatre, 1883.

Fake Beards

The style and value of the wig in ancient Egypt indicated the wearer's status in a hierarchical society. Wealthy people had many wigs, while the less well-off made do with one wig at a time. Very high-ranking women, such as the female pharaoh Hatshepsut, were sometimes portrayed wearing not only a wig but also a fake beard – a unique way to demonstrate they wielded the same authority as men.

Since the seventeenth century geisha have worn a special hairstyle, called the *shimada*, a traditional chignon with variations according to rank. But these traditional styles are a dying art and most modern geisha wear wigs rather than style their own hair.

Japanese Kabuki theatre, a highly stylised form of drama, relies on heavy makeup and unusual wig styles, either worn up or loose and long.

Classical Greek and Roman Wigs

In ancient Greece, where natural hair was regarded as sacred, both men and women often wore elaborate wigs on formal occasions. For a dinner party, for example, the wealthy showed off by decorating their wigs – sometimes in bright colours – with silver or gold jewellery, or rare fresh flowers.

Under the Roman Empire, short, neat, natural hair was favoured for men, but it was preferable to have a good head of hair. Julius Caesar was apparently embarrassed by his baldness and would either comb what little hair remained forward or wear a wig to disguise it. More often, however, the first emperor of Rome settled for a laurel wreath.

Roman women were admired for their bountiful locks but, to achieve this look, they often wore hairpieces and braids made of human hair to boost their elaborately plaited and coiled hairstyles.

Left: An ancient Greek sculpture of a woman, from about 530 BC, showing a typical wig of long kinked hair. Greek women also wore their hair in more complicated styles, often including plaits that were held in place with pins and other adornments.

The Return of the Wig

After the fall of the Roman Empire, wigs were not seen again until Elizabeth I of England – to conceal the fact that her own naturally red hair had turned white – started wearing tightly curled red wigs studded with pearls.

When Louis XIII of France went bald at quite a young age, he too began to wear a wig. His successor Louis XIV, who suffered from the same affliction, shaved off his hair and took to wearing wigs of ever-increasing size and elaboration. Naturally, his male courtiers were required to follow suit, and the periwig, a style also favoured by the English King Charles II and his court, was born.

The Periwig

Worn only by men, the periwig or peruke was an impressive wig of big, rigid curls, falling to below the shoulders and adding considerably to the wearer's height. The effect was rather like a lion's mane with a tight perm.

Above: A portrait, c.1700, of a gentleman in a substantial periwig. The best periwigs were made of human hair, although goat and horsehair were also used.

Above: In ancient Rome women's hairstyles changed so rapidly that a woman having her portrait sculpted might ask the artist to make her hairdo a detachable piece so it could be replaced with a more fashionable one if necessary. Tight curls, mounted on a wire frame, was a popular style of the era.

Ladies of Pleasure

Roman prostitutes were obliged by law to either wear a yellow wig or dye their hair yellow. The yellow dye made their hair fall out, so they tended to wear wigs anyway. The rather wild Empress Messalina (17–48 AD) owned a collection of yellow wigs she would wear on her nightly visits to a brothel.

Some years later, when yellow and blonde wigs became all the rage for respectable women trying to affect a fashionable 'tarty look', smart Roman ladies would have their wigs made from the hair of blonde German slaves.

The early Christians disapproved of wig-wearing. In the first century AD, theologian Clement of Alexandria declared that if somebody wearing a wig received a blessing, the blessing would benefit the wig, not the wearer. Cyprian, the Bishop of Carthage in the third century AD, wrote that 'adultery is a grievous sin, but she who wears false hair is guilty of a greater'.

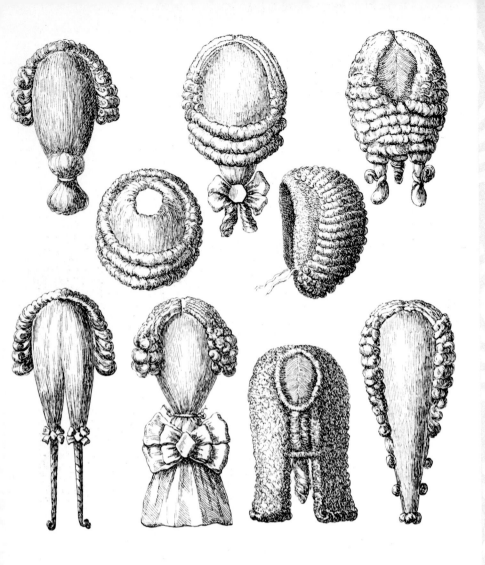

Above: A collection of eighteenth-century wig styles for men and women. Men's wigs often featured a tied queue at the back (see the top row, far left), which was called the English campaign wig.

Wig Raiders

As the leaders of society competed to be seen in the latest wig style, wig-makers began to charge extremely high prices for a wig made from human hair, rather than the alternative of cheaper animal hair. A large coloured and curled periwig represented a considerable investment. Not surprisingly, wig thieves began to prey on the fashionable gentry. Some thieves specialised in robbing passengers travelling in hackney coaches – they would ride up on horseback, cut an opening in the back of the cabin, grab a wig or two, then ride off at speed.

Bald Domes

In the seventeenth century, once wearing big wigs became *de rigueur* for most men, it was fashionable to have your own hair clipped short or completely shaved off. As men had been used to wearing their hair long, having it shaved for the first time could be traumatic. The English diarist Samuel Pepys, after watching his own locks falling to the floor, said it 'went to my heart at present to part with it'. But one thing Pepys said he would not miss were the lice with which so many heads were infested at the time – a wig was much easier to keep pest-free!

Winsome Wigs

During the first half of the eighteenth century, the smaller 'bob wig' and 'queue wig' for men came into fashion, although some older men continued to wear the periwig. The bob wig featured only a few rows of curls on each side, while the queue wig had a little tail at the back.

Until white and grey became the fashionable colours for all wigs, periwigs were styled with 'pomade' or styling wax and sometimes dusted over with powder in order to reduce the stickiness. Thus it became necessary to be heavy-handed with matching powder to achieve a matte effect. Powdering wigs became a highly skilled part of the barber's trade. For parties and special occasions, however, the white powder might be coloured pastel blue or pink, orange or lilac.

Because the wig powder was made from wheat flour, critics of powdering branded it a frivolous waste of an essential food product. Later in the century, both poor harvests and food shortages gave weight to this view. Finally, in 1795, the government introduced a tax on hair powder. To use it, you first had to buy a permit – at a cost of one guinea a year.

Some thieves specialised in robbing passengers travelling in hackney coaches – they would ride up on horseback, cut an opening in the back of the cabin, grab a wig or two, then ride off at speed.

Above: The relatively modest style of this gentleman's wig is offset by the enormous black bow used to tie his queue.

Right: In this eighteenth-century Swiss cartoon, the older man barely recognises the bewigged dandy his son has become.

Opposite: An Augustín Esteve portrait of Maria Teresa Apodaca de Sisma, whose massive wig looks as if it is mounted on some sort of frame.

Below: In this Gainsborough portrait, Mrs William Villebois wears the pompadour style, topped with feathers.

Right: A 1652 Velásquez portrait of Maria Anna (1634–1696) of Austria. The queen's wig is dressed to stick out on either side of her head, rather like the skirts in her farthingale.

To accommodate her hairstyles, Marie Antoinette had some doorways in Versailles Palace raised, while her hairstylist Leonard designed styles that could be disassembled for a carriage ride.

By the early 1800s, nobody fashionable wore a wig, and only older people persisted with powder. The era of the wig was over.

Left: 'The disastrous effects of the fashion conscious' – this eighteenth-century French illustration depicts a towering wig. Note the menagerie contained therein.

Mouse or Myth?

There are many stories of the amazing hairstyles and wigs worn by eighteenth-century women. Tales of ladies in tall wigs becoming wedged in doorways because their hair was too tall. Stories of society beauties with whole bouquets of flowers on their heads, complete with handy vases of water concealed within the hairstyle. Caricatures of Marie Antoinette with a model ship in her hair. It's even said that one could buy a wig with a built-in chandelier!

Sadly, most of these bizarre styles are fictional, depicted by contemporary cartoonists only in order to satirise the rich and fashionable. It's likely that only a few of these outrageous hairdos were specially created for a particular occasion, simply to attract attention. The styles actually worn by fashion leaders were certainly high and elaborate, but not as tall or heavily accessorised as legend would have it.

According to another well-known story, mice would nest in the wigs! But this was unlikely to have happened unless the wig was unworn for a long time, as these rodents tend not to nest in something that is constantly picked up, put on somebody's head and worn on the street!

Elaborate Arrangements

Although some eighteenth-century ladies wore full wigs and had whole collections in different styles, many of these hairstyles were achieved with a combination of padding, hairpieces and their natural hair, mainly because

Left: Imagine a hairstyle so tall – at least in this cartoonist's imagination – that you needed a sextant to navigate it?

Below left: Sometimes special bellows were used to douse a wig in as much as 500 g (1 lb) of flour. A cone to protect the wearer's respiratory tract was essential.

they wanted to keep their own long hair, and certainly wouldn't have been prepared to cut or shave it all off in order to make a wig fit better, as the men did. Lovely long hair was much prized at the time; a woman with short hair would have been pitied as someone who had obviously just been ill.

So, those cartoons of women in towering hairstyles, adorned with anything from a bunch of roses to a battleship in full sail, are probably not all showing a lady in a wig. It's quite likely that a maid had spent some time dressing Madam's own hair, attaching horsehair pads and hairpieces made of human hair and adding plenty of styling waxes and pomades to make the whole thing stay in place for the duration of a dinner party, or a night at the opera.

Needless to say, the most elaborate hairdos were so labour-intensive that they were reserved for wealthy women who could afford a lady's maid.

Revolution and Taxes

Two things put an end to both wigs and powder. First, the Reign of Terror during the French Revolution filled the working classes with resentment against their rulers, and wigs, those obvious badges of status, were hastily abandoned by anyone who wanted to keep their head. Republican hair, of course, was both uncoloured and unpowdered.

A couple of years later, the cash-strapped British government applied a tax to hair powder (see 'Profitable Powder', left). Most chic British folk immediately decided that powdered hair was no longer smart. By the early 1800s, nobody fashionable wore a wig and only older people persisted with powder. The era of the wig was over.

Profitable Powder

The wearing of wigs in Britain was to come to a rather peremptory end when the government suddenly recognised a highly profitable source of revenue, and levied a tax of 1 guinea a year on wig powder. Wigs had already been abandoned in the more democratic United States and, in France, where they had seemed to express the decadence of Louis XVI's court. It was to be the end of an era in Britain, and of a time when most of the population had become accustomed to wearing their aspirations firmly secured upon their heads.

Big Hair

During the Middle Ages and the Renaissance, women were expected to keep their hair modestly covered, especially once they were married. Again, it was Elizabeth I of England who defied convention – as the 'Virgin Queen', she kept her hair uncovered until later in life, inspiring other women to show their hair in all its glory. But that didn't mean the styles had to be modest and demure.

Top: The fontange is the term usually given to this tall headdress but in fact it applies only to the ribbons holding up the frelange, the actual framework. A tall mass of hair in front of the frelange was the crowning touch.

Opposite (top): Frothy curls and side ringlets feature in this seventeenth-century portrait.

Opposite (bottom): Various ringlet styles feature in this illustration from *La Mode Illustrée*, 1860.

Girls with Curls

While seventeenth-century men were having their heads shaved and donning elaborate periwigs, women were also creating impressive collections of curls and waves on their heads, all created from their own hair.

Ringlets had been known since Roman times, and probably before. They were formed by twisting the hair around a rag before going to sleep, or winding it around a heated curling iron while awake. For much of the seventeenth century, women wore big bunches of long ringlets on either side of their faces, with a bun, decorated with ribbons or braids, at the back. Unsuccessful versions of this style resembled the ears of spaniels, also fashionable at the court of Charles II of Spain.

The Fontange

The fontange was named after the Marquise de Fontanges, a mistress of Louis XIV of France. Marie Angélique was young, beautiful, extravagant and stupid, and she didn't last long as the king's favourite, as she died at the age

of 20, supposedly in childbirth, although it was whispered that she had been poisoned. The term 'fontange' often refers to a tall starched lace headdress worn just above the forehead, in front of a tall pile of hair, but technically it is the collection of ribbons adorning it. It was fashionable between 1690 and 1710.

The Pompadour

This style was named after Madame de Pompadour, mistress of Louis XV and one of history's great trendsetters, who inspired fashions in dress, interior decoration, architecture, porcelain, silk fabrics and more. Strangely enough, the pompadour style does not appear in any of her portraits; instead she wears a rather modest style.

A pompadour refers to any hairstyle, for both men or women, that is bouffant and swept back from the forehead. Since the eighteenth century, it has been in and out of fashion; it was popular for women in the Edwardian era, and then for men in the early days of rock'n'roll in the 1950s. And heavily greased, it's now a typical hairstyle for gangsters in Japanese popular culture.

The Quiff

The quiff, which emerged in the 1950s, evolved from the pompadour for men (the word 'quiff' probably derives from 'coiffure'). Rock'n'roll fans wore it in imitation of popular singers such as Elvis Presley, combing back the hair at the sides, close to the head, but keeping it long and bouffant on top. The peak could be about 5 cm (2 in) above the forehead. The style could only be maintained with hair creams, and cool young men always carried a comb so they could touch up their quiff, preferably in public. This look has been revived at various times in retro subcultures, such as Rockabilly, which was popular in the 1980s.

Through the late 1950s the quiff remained popular with Teddy Boys, who wore it with thick crepe-soled shoes, a wide draped jacket and very narrow 'drainpipe' trousers. The result was a distinctive silhouette. Biker-style clothes appeared increasingly with the hairstyle as, in the 1960s, Teddy Boys were superseded by Rockers, who had a less strict dress code but who still wore the quiff. The style was later ousted, even for Rockers, by the long shaggy hair that was typical of the late 1960s and 1970s.

The Mohawk

Another music-based style with a political edge, the Mohawk hairstyle became fashionable after the late 1970s Punk movement swept through youth culture, mainly in Europe and the United States, leaving fans dressed in black and studded with safety pins, sporting outrageous hairstyles that were tinted with rather luridly coloured dyes.

Above left: The British entertainer Cliff Richard adopts the classic pose of the 1950s quiff wearer as he combs back his hair – somewhat unnecessarily – at the sides.

Above: A young British man wears the modern Mohawk or Mohican, the classic Punk style – his head shaved except for the spine-like ridge of hair, 1982.

The Mohican or Mohawk hairstyle, originally derived from the traditional style worn by Native American Iroquois warriors, was popular for both male and female Punks, who teased their hair into rigid spiky shapes held in place with sugar water. The hair on the sides of their heads was either shaved or clipped short.

In the 1990s this initially rebellious and rather intimidating style became a tourist attraction in London, with remaining Mohican-wearers being photographed by eager tourists.

Fringe

The fringe, or bangs as it is called in the United States, has come and gone. In ancient Rome and Regency Britain, the forerunner of the fringe proper was a promenade of tight curls perched high on the forehead, but by the 'Swinging Sixties' it could be loose and long, or severe and straight, even cut asymmetrically, to complement the simple dress shapes that were popular at the time. Now it can be long – and impede vision – or swept to the side.

Right: Fashion designer Mary Quant has her hair cut in a rather severe geometric style by Vidal Sassoon, 1964.

Left: In World War II, when clothing and fabric were strictly rationed, women paid more attention to their hair, often wearing it formed into sausage-like 'Victory rolls'.

The slightly tousled 'sex kitten' look, epitomised by actresses such as Brigitte Bardot and Ann-Margret in the 1960s, gave the impression that the woman had only just raised her head from the pillow after a night of passion.

Left: Ann-Margret, perhaps best known for her role in *Bye Bye Birdie* (1963), was a so-called 'sex kitten' who wore her strawberry blonde hair long and wavy. To achieve the waves and also raise her hair from her forehead and temples, large curlers would have been used.

The Afro

During the 1960s, the rise of Black consciousness inspired many young people of African descent to look for hairstyles that would proclaim their heritage, rather than try to straighten their hair to conform with the fashions of other races. Straightening hair, which involved using strong chemicals, could be dangerous, and there had been some nasty accidents when earlier generations of African-Americans tried to straighten their hair.

The Afro or 'natural hair' style was achieved by growing the hair out so that it formed a cloud around the head. Men tended to wear the Afro shaped into a symmetrical 'globe' shape, while women preferred to wear longer and looser styles. The essential element was to leave the hair with its natural 'frizzy' or 'nappy' look, but an Afro was high-maintenance – it had to be shaped with styling products and also conditioned to avoid excessive dryness, and special wide-toothed Afro combs had to be used to avoid tangles. Afro styles and wigs were hugely popular throughout the 1970s and into the 1980s, especially in the United States.

Another traditional style revived by African-Americans at about this time was 'cornrow braids', which became fashionable for white girls for a while.

Dreadlocks

In the Caribbean, from the 1950s, followers of Rastafarianism began wearing dreadlocks – worn mainly by men – as a public statement of both their faith and heritage. The style was inspired by warriors of the Maasai people and other African tribes, who grew their hair into matted locks, sometimes dyed red. Similar, very long, locks are also worn by Hindu holy men. For Rastafarians, the mane-like style symbolises both their African heritage and the Lion of Judah, an important tenet in their religion.

Dreadlocks are created by letting the hair grow long without combing it out. The hair has to be separated into strands, then deliberately tangled at the roots and often backcombed within each strand to make it form a strongly matted strip of hair. Each lock may be rolled between the palms of the hands to create a rounded shape.

Above left: The African-American singer Marsha Hunt wears her hair in a natural style – the Afro, 1970.

Above: During World War II, Veronica Lake was asked to change her famous draped hairstyle after women kept getting their long hair caught in machines.

Left: In 1991, the American musician Lenny Kravitz wore loose dreadlocks, but a Rasta man often encloses his locks in a distinctive hat.

Loose and Lovely

The slightly tousled 'sex kitten' look, epitomised by actresses such as Brigitte Bardot and Ann-Margret in the 1960s, gave the impression that the woman had only just raised her head from the pillow after a night of passion. It may have required a head full of curlers and a session under a dryer, but long, carelessly arranged hair *looked* natural.

It was then a relatively short leap to the Hippy era of the late 1960s and early 1970s, when both men and women wore their hair long and loose, often with a centre parting. By the mid- to late 1970s, however, men graduated to the 'shag', a layered style to the collar that looked slightly dishevelled.

P703-168

Backcombing or teasing is a centuries-old technique for adding more bulk to the hair.

The Eton Crop, the Shingle and the Bob

There was a fashion revolution after World War I, when European women did something they had never done before in recorded history – they wore their skirts above their knees and cut their hair short. And not just short, but very, very short. The Eton crop, which scandalised respectable Britain, was essentially a boy's haircut, a 'short back and sides', with only a little extra length on top to distinguish it from the cut that your younger brother would wear back to school – Eton, of course. To soften it a little, flattened curls might be trained to sit on the forehead and at the sides.

The shingle was less extreme but drastic enough for women who had been used to growing waist-length hair. The sides were left long enough to form waves and curls around the ears, but the back was cut very short. Smart girls sometimes went to a men's barber for these cuts, as the women's salons didn't know how to cut the hair that short!

The bob – with the hair cut to about jaw-length, usually with a fringe – was made hugely popular by 1930s film stars and is still the basis for many hairstyles today. With either a centre or side part, it can look sleek and stylish.

Backcombing and Beehives

Backcombing or teasing is a centuries-old technique for adding more bulk to the hair. By holding up a section of hair and combing it back towards the roots, you can create an airy tangle that both lifts and supports the section of hair before you smoothe over the top of each section to create the desired style.

Backcombing became immensely popular for women in the 1950s and 1960s, first to create 'Italianate' styles, including the beehive, then later for the typical Mod girl's smooth, helmet-like bob. The '50s Italian look was teamed with pencil skirts, stiletto heels,

Opposite: American actress Louise Brooks wears her trademark bob, a style that requires precision cutting, 1928.

Right: A woman wrestles with teased sections of her own hair as well as hairpieces to achieve a 1960s up-do.

Below: The Ronettes, a 1960s African-American pop group, wearing straight-haired wigs in the latest beehive style.

drinking coffee and riding Vespa scooters. Big hair was required for a sexy look and was either worn long but backcombed to give height and a fashionably tousled appearance, or put up into a simple pleat at the back with plenty of backcombing on top. This gave a shape similar to the quiff for men (see page 214), but higher. Sometimes a few long ringlets were left to fall beguilingly over the shoulders.

The backcombed hair tended to form a conical shape called the beehive, a look that has often been revived by admirers of 1960s style. Hairdressers disapprove, as backcombing damages the hair, but for some fashionistas achieving the right look is worth it!

Colours & Curls

These days a new haircut is a short-lived transformation that can grow out quite quickly, but the creation of some so-called permanent styles – whether by streaking, perming, highlighting or dyeing – may require some more extreme measures.

Top: An electric curling tong heater with tongs, used in the 1890s to create waved hair, which was then piled on top of the head.

Above: The most famous peroxide blonde of all time – the naturally brown-haired Marilyn Monroe in *Gentlemen Prefer Blondes* (1953).

Blondes Have more Fun

In Renaissance Venice, golden hair was so prized that a lady would sit on her rooftop terrace, wearing a special crownless sunhat so she could spread her hair out on the brim to bleach in the sun. To aid this blonding process, a paste of white wine and olive oil was painted onto the hair.

Until relatively recently, the only hair dyes available were plant extracts, such as henna and indigo. These are effective dyes but the results are rather hard to control – henna can turn hair orange while indigo dyes it dark blue.

In the twentieth century, the Hollywood star machine promoted popular performers, convincing the public that – with Marilyn Monroe's not inconsiderable help – 'blondes have more fun'. At the time, crude chemicals became available for home bleaching, and many aspiring film stars bleached their hair until it split and fell off.

From the late 1970s and into the 1980s Punk hairstyles (see page 214), could be coloured bright red, blue, purple or green.

Streaking

It all started with the iconic up-do in *Breakfast at Tiffany's* (1961) – Audrey Hepburn's elegant style featured random golden streaks through her own brown hair. Suddenly, everybody wanted streaks, and the fashion has endured, although now they're more often called 'highlights and lowlights'.

At first, the only way to have streaks done at a hairdressing salon was to wear a hideous rubber cap riddled with holes, through which strands of hair were pulled with a crochet hook before they were bleached. This process could be extremely painful.

In the twentieth century the Hollywod star machine promoted popular performers, convincing the public that – with Marilyn Monroe's not inconsiderable help – 'blondes have more fun'.

These days streaks are a painless but still elaborate, and expensive, process, as the coloured or bleached sections are individually wrapped in metal foil while the colour develops. Apprentice hairdressers spend hours of their lives preparing these little sections of foil for the day's clients! The usual aim is to make the hair look as if it's been naturally lightened by the sun, but some people go for something braver or more exotic, such as a purple streak. Bolder stripe-like streaks can easily be achieved with modern bleaches, but of course you do run the risk of ending up looking like a badger!

Right: Rita Hayworth, an American actress of the 1940s, dyed her famous hair red and used electrolysis to raise her hairline.

Below: Wearing a Givenchy dress, a tiara perched in her streaked beehive – Audrey Hepburn in character as Holly Golightly in *Breakfast at Tiffany's*, 1961.

'Permament Waves'

Invented in the late nineteenth century, the 'Permanent Wave' – or perm – did not become popular until the twentieth century. A perm involves several stages – first, you apply a chemical lotion, which breaks down the structure of the hair, then you wind the hair onto heated rollers of the desired size and 'cook' them into shape. Once the style was deemed ready, you applied a second lotion to halt the process.

Early perms involved being hooked up to a terrifying machine that heated the rollers, while being doused in perm lotions with a strong chemical smell. Women preferred this somewhat unpleasant experience to sleeping with rollers in their hair or using primitive curling tongs. A perm was really the only way to achieve the fashionable flat curls of the 1920s and early 1930s.

By the mid-twentieth century, women could buy a home perm. For years a famous series of advertisements, featuring pairs of twins, asked: 'Which twin has the Toni?'. The company claimed that the results looked the same as a professional salon perm.

In the 1970s, most men were wearing longer hair, and perms became popular for fashionable males. All-over curls were favoured by footballers, for some reason, and perms were also applied to the notorious 'mullet' hairstyle – short on top and long at the back.

Curling Tools

It seems that people with straight hair always want to have curly hair, and vice versa. As hair is obstinate stuff, altering its natural behaviour can be quite a brutal procedure.

Curling tongs go back a long way. Made of iron, they would be heated up in the fire before a lock of hair was wound around them to form a curl. It was a slow process and had an unfortunate tendency to melt the hair.

During the twentieth century, new curling tongs, which used electricity or butane gas, became available. These were less prone to disaster and much quicker to use, although it was still easy to over-cook the hair or even inflict small burns on the face.

One traditional way to straighten wavy hair was to use a household iron, perhaps with a sheet of brown paper protecting the hair. This would produce dead straight hair, usually with split ends, as it was dried out by the iron. Again, using electric straighteners made life a lot easier.

Crimpers were popular in the Hippy era. They produce a ridged effect by baking small waves into the hair.

Opposite: In the 1960s large curlers were required for achieving a bouffant hairdo.

Below left: A perming machine in action, 1937.

Below: A perm sometimes required crimping horizontal sections of hair with long clamps.

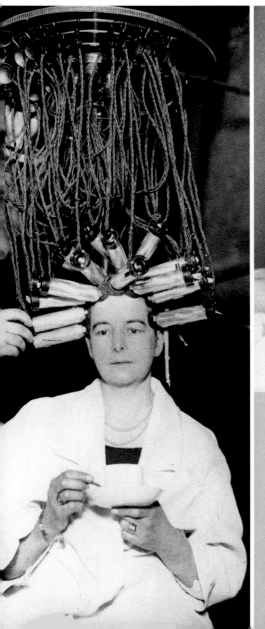

One traditional way to straighten wavy hair was to use a household iron, perhaps with a sheet of brown paper protecting the hair.

Facial Hair

Some generations celebrate facial hair with beards, moustaches and monobrows, while others try to remove it altogether, plucking it out hair by tedious hair – perhaps yet another example of the well-to-do trying to impress upon the working classes the pointlessness of having so much leisure time.

The Hairless Face

Trendsetters throughout history have all agreed that women look smarter with shaped eyebrows and no stray facial hairs. At times, however, this trend has been taken to extremes.

In the Middle Ages, European women valued the high forehead and hairless face, achieved by either plucking out the hair or killing it off with a mixture of cat faeces and vinegar. The eyebrows would be removed, and perhaps drawn in only very lightly with pale makeup; extreme fashionistas would also pluck out their eyelashes. Short hairs around the neck and sides of the face would be removed, so that not one hair showed under the elaborate headdressess.

Above: In the eighteenth century one's toilette was an elaborate procedure, requiring a walnut and silver gilt dressing case.

Right: This fifteenth-century Flemish portrait shows extreme hair plucking, a rather nude look below the fashionable tall headdress.

Mournful Eyebrows

Ancient Egyptian women used sugar paste to remove their eyebrows and any stray facial hair, repainting their eyebrows with kohl to achieve a perfect shape. To remove the eyebrows without painting them back on was a sign of mourning; it was believed that, when a cat died, every member of the feline's family mourned its passing by doing this.

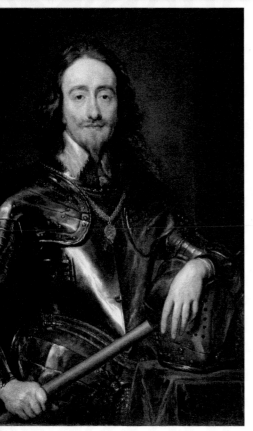

Above: The original 'It Girl', the American film actress Clara Bow, her hair softly curled and her own brows plucked and replaced with new, mournful ones, according to the fashion of the 1920s and '30s.

Left: Charles I of England, in a seventeenth-century portrait by Sir Anthony van Dyck, wearing a moustache and a goatee or 'van Dyck' beard with shaven cheeks.

In contrast, in classical Rome heavy eyebrows were admired so much that the monobrow – the eyebrows joining above the nose – became fashionable.

Beards and Moustaches

Facial hair has always allowed men to express either their individuality or their ability to be 'on trend', and through the centuries the styles and lengths of facial hair have varied enormously.

Moustaches, once they've been grown more than a certain length, have to be treated with wax to keep their shape, and they may also be styled to turn up at the ends. Elongated moustaches that drooped down at the side of the mouth were worn in ancient China, but these days many Chinese believe that wearing a moustache brings bad luck.

The handlebar moustache, for instance, was frequently worn in seventeenth-century Europe, usually combined with a small goatee or van Dyck, or van Dyke, beard. The handlebar came back into fashion during World War II, when pilots in the British Royal Air Force wore it without the beard.

In recent centuries full beards, usually worn by those actually spurning the fashion of the day, have rarely been on trend; a notable exception was the Hippy beard. But in the mid-Victorian era, facial hair of all kinds was highly admired and, to modern eyes, the results often look unpleasantly woolly. A more moderate style in this period was the charmingly named mutton chop whiskers, with long sideburns extending to meet a full moustache.

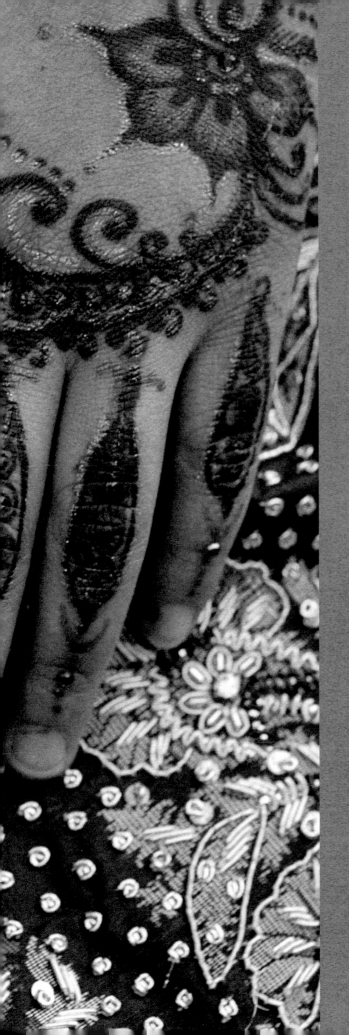

9
body art

The universality
of tattooing is a
curious subject for
speculation. JAMES COOK, 1728–1779

Body Painting
& Colouring

The body may be a temple, but it's often a highly decorated one. Since the Stone Age human beings have used their bodies as a canvas – painting, dyeing and tanning their skin according to certain traditions. Usually these techniques have religious or social significance but – unlike tanning – they don't have the potential to shorten your life.

Above: An Egyptian noblewoman, duly plucked and painted, and wearing a cone of perfumed tallow on her head (see page 156), requires assistance to prepare her toilette.

Ancient Egyptians

As we know, the fashionable ancient Egyptians were strongly opposed to body hair. Having removed it all, they would sometimes adorn their bodies with paint – for instance, outlining veins in blue, or painting their nipples gold (if the nipples weren't actually exposed, they could probably be seen through their fine white linen garments).

About That Famous Woad

Some cultures have traditionally coloured their bodies in a more lasting way than just with paint, using plant or chemical dyes – a practice which has continued up to the present day.

Left: In India, an intricate design is applied with henna, dispensed from a plastic bag. Sugar and oil are used to help fix the colour.

Opposite bottom: This gentle, romantic sixteenth century portrait, called *A Young Daughter of the Picts*, may well be a fanciful interpretation of how the Picts decorated their bodies.

An early recorded example is the tribe the Romans called *Picti,* meaning 'painted people', who lived in eastern and northern Scotland in ancient times. The colonising Romans had to deal with fierce guerrilla warfare from the Picts, who were tough, hairy and blue.

The blue colour is famous as having come from the plant woad, which the tribespeople are said to have used to make a dye that they rubbed all over their bodies. In fact, woad is not a very effective dye for skin, although it works well on textiles.

It's more likely that the Picts extracted dyes from earth containing high levels of copper or iron, which, although ultimately toxic, would have given a better colour. Certainly these substances were all dyes, not paints,

so the tint on the skin would have been semi-permanent.

Julius Caesar actually said that all the British were blue, so it was either a more widespread custom at the time when he first invaded, or it was a *very* cold day.

Mehndi

Like woad, henna is a plant extract, and an effective dye for applying to the hair and body. While it's not permanent, the stain that henna leaves on the skin can be long-lasting, remaining for up to three weeks.

Mehndi, a traditional form of body art in India, Pakistan and Bangladesh, involves using henna to draw designs on the body. Widely used for weddings and other celebrations in India and

parts of the Middle East, some mehndi decorations are only for women, but in other areas men are decorated too. The parts of the body most often decorated are the hands and feet, but designs can also be drawn on the chest, neck and even the face.

Although some symbolic designs, such as the sun, are used, mehndi designs are mostly just decorative, often swirling leaf and plant motifs. After the designs are painted on, they are covered for a few hours to help the colour develop. It then takes another day or so before the henna turns a nice rich brown. Having the mehndi designs applied for a wedding is a celebration in itself, sometimes involving hundreds of people as the bride and her family and friends are all decorated together.

Above: These figures – a detail of the decorated gold throne of the pharaoh Tutankhamun – show the deep ochre colour of ancient Egyptian body paint.

...having a tan indicated that you worked as a manual labourer in the open air, so it was considered low-class and not the least bit chic.

Tanning

Those ancient Egyptians were ahead of their time again: some of them tinted their bodies orange or yellow all over, in an interesting forerunner of the modern fake tan. But until the twentieth century there's no other recorded instance of tanning being fashionable. Great warriors or explorers might have been admired, but no one wanted to imitate their weatherbeaten looks. Besides, having a tan indicated that you worked as a manual labourer in the open air, so

it was considered low-class and not the least bit chic. Marie Antoinette played at being a shepherdess on her model farm, but she wouldn't have dreamed of having a sun-browned face.

It was the great trendsetter, the French designer Coco Chanel, who turned it all around in the late 1920s when she returned from a holiday on the French Riviera with a bad case of sunburn. Her fans imitated her, and suddenly a tan became a sign that you were a privileged member of the leisured classes.

Unfortunately, until the links between tanning and premature ageing of the skin as well as skin cancer were recognised, the tan had become firmly established as a glamorous necessity.

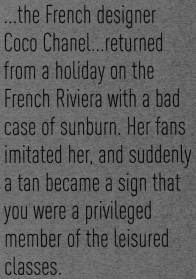

...the French designer Coco Chanel...returned from a holiday on the French Riviera with a bad case of sunburn. Her fans imitated her, and suddenly a tan became a sign that you were a privileged member of the leisured classes.

Above left: The influential French fashion designer Coco Chanel, pictured in Paris in 1929, is credited with 'inventing' the tan.

Above: A 1950s bathing belle applies suntan lotion. The process is like basting a roasting turkey but at least the bird can't develop skin cancer.

Assisted Tanning

Fake-tan lotions, first produced in the 1950s, were essentially skin dyes, and many of them contained henna, which meant that the skin of the careless could not only turn a noticeable orange but also emit a distinctive smell. Still, 'self-tanning' products were embraced by many people who couldn't easily achieve a natural tan, and they soon became very big business.

In the late twentieth century a craze for tanning on sunbeds caught on, and fashion victims baked themselves under ultraviolet light. Since then, with better knowledge about the damaging effects of UV rays, fans of the tan have begun to patronise spray-tan salons.

Skin Lightening

Meanwhile, some people with naturally brown skins apply products to lighten their skin tone, especially on the face. Some people with a South Asian background in particular – to resemble Bollywood film stars, who are mostly quite light-skinned – aim for a 'caramel' tone. These lightening products can damage the skin but, as ever, the risk is discounted in pursuit of the right look.

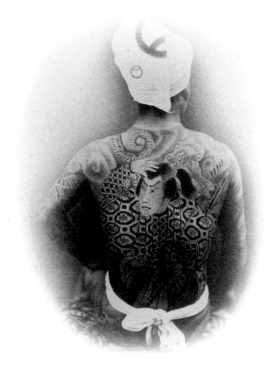

Tattooing

Whether small and discreet, visible to only a select few, or worn like a pair of all-in-ones, a tattoo is the ultimate form of personal adornment and, until recently, a permanent fashion accessory.

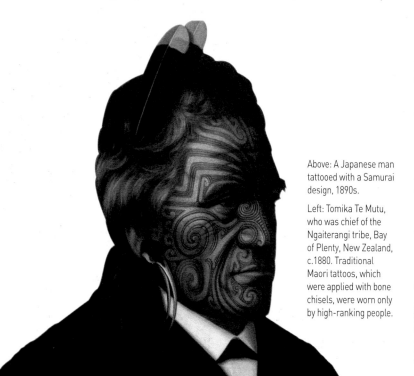

Above: A Japanese man tattooed with a Samurai design, 1890s.

Left: Tomika Te Mutu, who was chief of the Ngaiterangi tribe, Bay of Plenty, New Zealand, c.1880. Traditional Maori tattoos, which were applied with bone chisels, were worn only by high-ranking people.

Japanese *Irezumi*

Tattooing involves actually breaking the skin and inserting dye underneath. As the skin heals over, the dye forms a permanent mark, so having a tattoo done is a momentous act that changes your appearance for life.

Having a tattoo done is painful so, until recently, being tattooed has often been associated with being tough and even criminal. This is especially the case in Japan, where *Irezumi*, meaning 'inserting ink', has a long history. Highly fashionable at different periods in history, it was also used in early times to brand prisoners.

Japanese tattoos often completely cover an area of skin with a dense design. In the seventeenth century, some of the great woodblock artists would also use their skills to design elaborate tattoos that were worn by all, from merchants to firemen.

However, after tattooing was made illegal in the eighteenth century, it became associated with crime and the notorious *yakuza* gangsters, who favoured full-body *tebori* tattoos and facial designs. Even now that it's legal again, for many Japanese there is still a low-life connotation, and wearers of large tattoos are denied admittance to some gyms and swimming pools.

Polynesian *Tatau*

Although many cultures have a strong tattooing tradition, the Western world first became really aware of it when eighteenth-century explorers such as Captain James Cook encountered the islanders of the South Pacific, where *tatau* was an important art form. The sailors, returning home with tattooed bodies, were admired, and the exotic practice caught on.

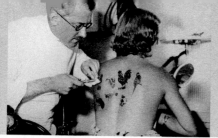

An early traveller mistook the tattoos on Samoan men – tattooed from waist to knee – for tight-fitting patterned silk breeches. Throughout the South Pacific, men and women were tattoed throughout their lives, with different designs symbolising life stages. In the nineteenth century, however, tattooing was strongly discouraged and even banned by missionaries. The traditions have only been revived in recent times, but modern islanders are usually less heavily tattooed than their ancestors.

The traditional tattoos of the Maoris and Polynesian islanders include a wide range of subtle abstract designs, many of which have symbolic meanings, now imitated by enthusiasts worldwide.

Modern 'Ink'

Tattoos became more widely accepted in the 1990s, then highly fashionable in the first years of the new century. The image of a tattoo completely changed, from 'I love Sally' in a blurred blue heart on the forearm of a retired mariner to a sharply executed modern 'tat', perhaps in Chinese characters or a Celtic design on the chest or back of a young person, in imitation of a style icon or film star.

Even conventional men and women began to sport tattoos and, in many Western countries, a visible tattoo became acceptable at most places of employment. This would not have been the case – especially for women – even ten years earlier. Sometimes fashion can overrule or dictate public opinion.

The sleeve tattoo involves covering the whole of the arm with either a single unified design or a series of smaller ones. 'Getting sleeved' requires a collaboration between the artist and the wearer, and involves perhaps weeks or even months of pain.

Above: A Parisienne acquires another tattoo for her lumbar menagerie before she hits the beach, 1934. The rooster is a rather curious inclusion.

Right: A peacock and skull design by Mike Rubendall, New York, 2008. The peacock – naturally very popular with men – has many meanings, while the skull may symbolise death, decay or a reminder to simply *carpe diem*, or seize the day.

Piercing

Making holes in your earlobes is a convenient way to secure your favourite pair of earrings, while securing objects in other parts of your body may signify certain religious or spiritual beliefs, or even membership of a subculture. Piercing can also be a political and social statement that coincidentally scares the hell out of your enemy, or your next-door neigbour.

Ancient Piercers

Body piercing – revived by the youth culture in the late twentieth century – has been around since ancient times. In Egypt noblemen would wear plugs in their ears, but only a pharaoh could sport a piercing in his navel. The Egyptians also displayed their wealth with heavy, elaborate gold and enamel earrings, which they believed enhanced their beauty.

Centurions in the armies of ancient Rome had pierced nipples – which symbolised strength and virility – as a badge of honour, while in Central America, both the Mayans and Aztecs treated tongue piercing as a religious ritual, believing that the blood letting involved in the procedure brought them closer to the gods.

Ear Piercing

Piercing the ears in order to hang jewellery in them is one of the most ancient and common ways to modify the body permanently in search of decoration and fashion. It's been fashionable for different types of

Top left: Persian gold earring, 600–400 BC.

Left: In a Greek freso from the sixteenth century BC a priestess wears large earrings.

Left: A Roman woman wears pearl drop earrings.

Below: The English explorer Sir Walter Raleigh, one of Elizabeth I's favourites, wears a pearl earring; the pearl symbolises purity.

In Central America, both the Mayans and the Aztecs treated tongue piercing as a religious ritual, believing that the blood letting involved in the procedure brought them closer to the gods.

people at different times – stylish young gentlemen at the court of Elizabeth I of England would wear one earring in a pierced ear, perhaps a pendant pearl. A sailor would wear one gold earring, which was said to be a handy payment for his funeral if he were drowned and washed up on a foreign shore. For women, pierced ears have at times been dismissed as low-class, but they've eventually come back into general fashion again.

Usually, the hole in the ear is just big enough to allow the wire of an earring to pass through. In some tribal societies the holes are made bigger and bigger over time, which is imitated in modern body piercing by the kind of earring known as a 'flesh tunnel' or 'spacer'.

Above: A young Punk woman. It was not unusual for Punks to pierce their ears, nose, mouth and cheeks.

Above right: A Bengali bride, her hands tattooed with henna, has a tiny piercing in her nostril.

Above left: In the late nineteenth century having pierced ears was an insurance policy against losing a valuable pair of earrings.

Left: A lip piercing.

Nose Piercing

A ring or stud in the nose is a traditional adornment for Indian women. A small stud is often placed in the left nostril as, according to Ayurvedic medicine, this part of the body is linked to the health of the female reproductive organs.

The Piercing Subculture

Until the late twentieth century, body piercing was virtually unknown in Western culture, except for a discreet subculture of people who favoured nipple and genital piercings, believed to enhance sexual pleasure. The Punk movement of the 1970s introduced a youth fashion for deliberately amateurish-looking piercings, often featuring safety pins or plain steel rings

(see page 103). Young people began to wear multiple piercings in their ears, graduating to piercing their eyebrows, lips and noses. The two subcultures combined to some extent, as piercing became widely available and more and more common, athough always predominantly among the young, reaching a peak in the 1990s.

As with tattooing, there seems to be an addictive or 'collecting' element to it, and very large numbers of piercings – up to several thousand – on the one body have been recorded. But it's been estimated that complications and infections occur in as many as 30 per cent of cases. Navel piercings are particularly prone to infection and often take a very long time to heal.

10
bend me, shape me

Fashion condemns us to many follies; the greatest is to make ourselves its slave. NAPOLEON BONAPARTE, 1769–1821

Body Binding

In the ancient cultures of Egypt and Rome, crunching bones was considered a small price to pay to acquire the perfectly shaped skull. Parents believed their children would thank them later in life for almost squeezing the life out of them as soon as they were born – provided, of course, that they lived to tell the tale.

Crushed into Shape

In the fourteenth century BC, Queen Nefertiti of Egypt was considered the archetype of female beauty, possessing flattened cheekbones and a domed forehead – a sign not only of her beauty and intelligence but also of her affinity with the spirit world.

In ancient Egypt the practice of head binding was seen as an essential rite of passage if one hoped to get on in the world. Parents often bound their children's heads with cloth when they were only a month old, or clamped their skulls between two wooden slats to produce the much desired elongated shape. The Romans too stretched and pulled their struggling infants, like obdurate blobs of plasticene, into the desired shape, binding their heads to ensure roundness.

Lotus Flowers

For a thousand years in China, girls as young as five were subjected to the terrifying ordeal of foot binding. Often the foot binder would be the child's own mother, determined to give her daughter what was considered her best chance of finding a wealthy husband. Equipped with a box containing a knife, long strips of cloth, needle and thread, she would place before her young victim a pair of tiny shoes, a heart-stopping 7 cm (2¾ in) long.

Winter was the season favoured for this rite of passage, as it was thought the cold would help to numb the pain of this excruciatingly painful procedure. The child's feet were soaked in some

Above left: With a name that literally means 'Perfect One', we could assume that the beauty and symmetry of Queen Nefertiti's well proportioned face was *not* idealised by the sculptor Thutmose.

Far left: A pair of Chinese shoes for a girl or woman with bound feet.

Left: Not only has foot binding reduced this woman's toes to a grotesque triangular shape but her heels look as if they belong on a pair of shoes.

warm water and a regular witch's brew of ingredients, such as ground almonds, mulberry roots, tannin, urine or boiled monkey bones. First the foot binder trimmed the toenails right back, then she folded the four smallest toes into the sole of the foot, actually breaking the arch and the toes as she did so. Finally, she bound them with the strips of cloth, which she tightened and sewed firmly into place. In the first months of having newly bound feet, small girls would weep each time they walked. Girls who endured foot-binding knew the painful truth of this old Chinese saying: 'A thousand buckets of tears for one who binds her feet'.

Eventually the pain gave way to numbness and, after two years of regular rebinding, when the toes were permanently folded in, the little girl could proudly slip her tiny 7-cm (2¾-in) long feet into the gorgeously embroidered slippers that were her reward.

Strict criteria governed the success of the foot binders in achieving their goal. Feet 10 cm (4 in) long merited the Silver Lotus but 7-cm (2¾-in) feet, considered perfection, earned the title of Golden Lotus. To achieve this standard, the bound foot had to seem like an extension of the leg.

Men were entranced by the idea of their wives being a symbol of their wealth and status, unable to work. Their hobbled feet meant that the women were their husbands' prisoners as surely as if they wore leg irons.

Right: A young Chinese woman rebinds her feet. The rich would have performed this ritual daily, while peasants would have done so at least twice a week.

Theatrical Inspiration

The practice of foot binding may have begun innocuously enough when a group of dancers performed at court during the ninth-century Tang dynasty. They had bound their feet with white silk to perform the story of an Indian princess whose feet were as delicate as a doe's and whose footprints resembled lotus flowers, a symbol of fecundity. The audience was riveted by the delicacy of those tiny feet, which seemed to express the very essence of femininity. Soon the ladies of the court began to imitate the dancers, tightly binding their feet so their footprints too might resemble lotus flowers.

Secrets of the Boudoir

Soon this fashion for tiny feet, regarded as a mark of refinement and sexual allure, spread from the elite of the royal court to all social classes. Red satin shoes were judged the height of fashion, contrasting as they did with the ghostly pallor of a woman's skin. Bound feet became the object of erotic fantasy, and sex manuals were written to assist those who wished to worship at their lover's swaddled toes. In a bizarre twist, the horror that often lay beneath the binding cloths seems to have fuelled the erotic charge.

There was a cruel price to pay for what were considered the delicacy and beauty of 'lotus feet'. Many women suffered appalling injuries. The bandages cut off the supply of blood, causing gangrene and fatal infections that led to nerve damage and amputation. In the seventeenth and eighteenth centuries the Manchu emperors tried to ban the practice but the widespread belief that, without tiny feet a woman could not attract a husband, meant their attempts were doomed to failure.

Ladies of the Manchu court who left their feet unbound were dismissed as ugly and, although they attempted to imitate the gait of women with bound feet by wearing 'flower bowl' platform shoes, they were mocked for being poor imitations of the real thing.

Escape from the Doll's House

It was not until the social upheaval following China's revolution of 1911 that foot binding was recognised as a crippling practice. At last women saw themselves as independent of their husbands. But so deeply ingrained was the tradition that it persisted in many regions, even though it now meant the foot binder had to be smuggled in at night.

The situation did not begin to change until 1928, when the Ministry of Domestic Affairs enforced the laws more vigorously. Fines were imposed and inspectors descended on villages, unbinding the feet of all girls younger than fifteen. Sadly, for the older ones, it was already too late. They faced a lifetime of debilitating health problems associated with their bound feet.

Dragon's Claws

According to Chinese tradition, long fingernails were intended, like the delicate lotus feet, to convey a woman's high status in society.

In the nineteenth century, Cixi, the Dowager Empress of China, whose humble birth did not prevent her from catching the emperor's eye, was a devotee of 10-cm (4-in) nails and left no one in any doubt that she was his favourite concubine. She followed ancient tradition by wearing long gold fingernail protectors on the ring and little fingers of one hand. To the servants who kept those nails in perfect decorative order behind the high walls of the Forbidden City, she must have been manicuring her way to power!

Above: A Chinese woman with so-called 'lotus feet', like a doe's hooves, c.1900.

Opposite: The third and fourth fingers of Cixi, the Dowager Empress of China, were reportedly 10 cm (4 in) long.

Perfect Proportions

The quest for physical perfection has led to an amazing array of medical procedures, and these days every conceivable part of the body, from brows to buttocks, seems capable of transformation. Thankfully, physical exercise is not only still popular but also achieves results – usually without breaking bones.

Above: In this eighteenth century French engraving, an older woman purchases a pair of plump prosthetic breasts to help fill her fashionable Empire line gown.

The First 'Strong Man'

In New York's Brooklyn in the early 1900s, Angelo Siciliano, a rather weedy individual who suffered from anaemia, made a discovery that changed his life. Unable to participate in sport, Siciliano spent his time at the Brooklyn Museum, where he would admire the perfectly developed, muscular bodies of the Greek and Roman statues. At Prospect Zoo he also noticed how restless lions retained their muscle tone in their cramped cages by continuous flexing.

The discovery inspired Siciliano to begin some dedicated muscle flexing of his own as he began to capitalise on the growing contemporary obsession with self-improvement.

By 1922 Siciliano had found work as a vaudeville strongman. He soon changed his name to Charles Atlas and set up a mail order business through a New York gymnasium. But it was a comic strip, suggested by an advertising executive, that made him a household name. 'Weedy Mac' – mocked when he bares his chest on the beach and rejected by his girlfriend – discovers the Charles Atlas Fitness Regime, beats the bully and wins back the girl.

Living in Air

New life was literally breathed into the program in the 1960s when Charles Atlas's 'dynamic tension' gave way to a new exercise craze called isometrics. The advent of the Industrial Age, with city dwellers sitting for long hours in offices, made the need for exercise even more urgent. Gymnasiums became the places where people hoped to tone their muscles and shed the extra weight.

'Engines of exercise' had been available in the 1890s but had looked alarmingly like machines of torture.

With machines like the motorised Slendo Ring Roller, it seemed that a toned figure could be achieved with the mere flick of a switch.

Left: Charles Atlas, flexing his muscles in about 1945, is responsible for the cliché 'the 97-pound weakling'.

Right: Betty Grable, in a still from the 1947 film *Mother Wore Tights*, shows off the beautifully proportioned legs that her studio had insured for $1,000,000 with Lloyds of London.

But the equipment that was popular in the 1960s was rather less intimidating and often pandered to the users' desire to avoid over-exerting themselves. With machines like the motorised Slendro Ring Roller, it seemed that a toned figure could be achieved with the mere flick of a switch.

It was another American, called Ben Cooper, who stumbled upon an exercise program that addressed the problem of an increasingly unfit population. A medic in the US Air Force, Cooper was convinced that an unfit heart and lungs could be strengthened by sustained strenuous effort. He called his training program 'aerobic' after the Greek term for 'living in air'.

Breaking the Mould

While plastic surgery came into its own in the 1960s as the search for the body beautiful became an obsession, the reshaping of the body for aesthetic purposes dates back to antiquity.

The word 'plastic' derives from the Greek *plastikos*, or mould. In ancient Egypt it was important to look good in the afterlife, so the noses of dead pharaohs were sometimes reshaped by the insertion of a small bone. The Romans, accustomed to exhibiting their naked bodies at public baths, used circumcision to correct any imperfections in that area.

But the advance of surgery of any kind was abruptly halted in the Middle Ages when the Church regarded the spilling of blood as a cardinal sin. In the late sixteenth century an Italian, Gasparo Taglacozza, regarded as the father of plastic surgery, succeeded in grafting skin from an arm to rebuild a nose. During the Counter-Reformation, however, such practices were again dismissed as heretical magic.

It was the advent of two world wars in the twentieth century – when doctors had to deal with horrific injuries – that led to huge advances in skin grafts and bone reconstruction and understanding tissue health. But when World War II ended, plastic surgeons, forced to seek patients elsewhere, began to target affluent middle-aged women.

Pearly Whites

Portraits of the rich and powerful through the ages share a common feature – the subjects rarely seem to smile. Queen Elizabeth I of England, elaborately be-wigged and gorgeously attired, is invariably depicted with her rosebud mouth clamped tightly shut, while Nell Gwynne, the beguiling mistress of Charles II, also of England, bared her shapely bosom but did not open her lips. Teeth, or the absence of them, were to prove an extraordinary leveller over the centuries, for kings and queens, nobles and society ladies all shared with the humblest peasant the curse of rotten teeth.

Above: A twentieth century copy of an Etruscan denture. The Estruscans made their bridges using gold, hence the gilding.

The First Dentures

The earliest attempts at dentures were ingenious. The first false teeth date back to Italy in 700 BC, when the Etruscans fashioned them out of ivory and bone and attached them to the mouth with gold bridges. The Chinese probably used acupuncture as early as 2700 BC to ease the agony of tooth decay, but it was not until the sixteenth century that the Japanese succeeded in producing a working set of dentures made from wood. But in Elizabethan England, where false teeth were rare, the antisocial problem of bad breath was combated by mouthwashes made of wine, alum, honey and sweet herbs.

'Waterloo Teeth'

The quest to produce the perfect set of false molars resulted in some creative solutions that benefited the wealthy. In the eighteenth century, dentists – known as Operators of Teeth, who were often goldsmiths or ivory turners – carved teeth from bone as well as elephant and hippopotamus ivory.

But the demand was highest for human teeth acquired from corpses, and battlefields provided the best opportunity for acquiring a generous supply. Once the fighting had ended, scavengers moved among the dead, using pliers to pull teeth, which they then sold for a huge profit. After the Battle of Waterloo in 1815, London's wealthy elite flashed what became known as 'Waterloo Teeth', the ultimate 'must have' accessory of the time.

While corpses from both the battlefield and the graveyard met the demand for teeth, healthy teeth from the poorest children in society could be bought for only a few pence and used for what were euphemistically described as 'live implants', claimed to last for ten years. As gap-toothed urchins roamed the streets, members of society showed off their implants.

Porcelain Perfection

Although human teeth continued to literally fill the gap, porcelain teeth became popular in the late eighteenth century after the French apothecary, Alexis Duchateau, perfected the first set of porcelain dentures. His assistant, Nicholas Dubois de Clémant, acquired the British patent in 1791, becoming licensed to make 'artificial teeth'. It proved a lucrative market. In England Josiah Wedgewood and Sons not only provided aristocrats with fine china for their tea tables but also porcelain teeth for their mouths.

Right: A full set of dentures made of hippopotamus ivory, sitting in a porcelain holder, c.1780–1820.

Below: 'The Transplanting of Teeth' by Thomas Rowlandson, a satirical look at removing teeth from the poor to benefit the wealthy.

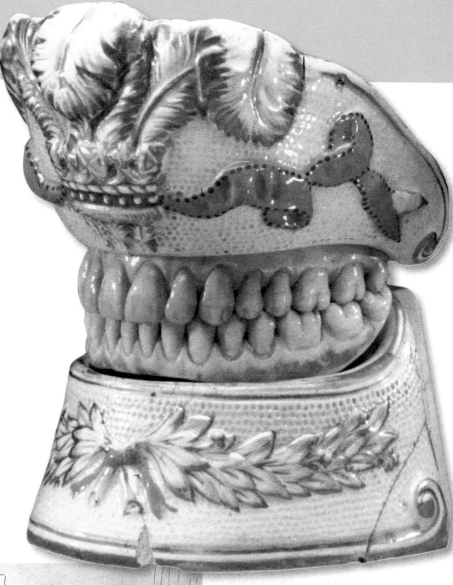

Soon extra refinements were added and, in 1820, an English goldsmith called Claudius Ash began mounting his porcelain dentures on an 18-carat gold plate. Later dentures were made of vulcanite, a form of hardened rubber, in which the teeth were set.

Among the members of high society the habit of removing dentures before eating had become an acceptable practice, although ladies tended to gulp down some food in their rooms before dinner, and would merely fiddle with their food at table rather than risk the embarrassment of their false teeth splashing into the soup.

Women seeking a husband had to be particularly cautious, pursing their lips in their efforts not to kill the romance stone dead.

Left: For centuries blacksmiths and barbers performed tooth extractions in public, as in this marketplace in the Netherlands, painted in 1645.

Dentures Make the Difference

Through the centuries the quality of their dentures would come to distinguish a wealthy elite, with an open-lipped smile considered the ultimate goal.

Women seeking a husband had to be particularly cautious, pursing their lips in their efforts not to kill the romance stone dead. The notion that their own teeth might survive their lifetime seemed a distant fancy until the latter half of the twentieth century. Sadly, a wedding present often given to young women, right up until the 1950s, was the removal of all their teeth and the fitting of dentures.

Anaesthetic Addicts

The agony of tooth extraction could not be avoided, even by the haute monde. *The first local anaesthetic, cocaine, was not used until the late nineteenth century, and had the unfortunate side effect of turning patients into addicts. Non-addictive novocaine replaced it in 1905, as concern for dental health rather than fashion became the driving force.*

Monarchs in the past would have happily embraced this option, however. Louis XIV of France and Elizabeth I of England both had to make important decisions while suffering agony from their troublesome molars. And Winston Churchill's World War II speeches would not have rallied the spirits of the nation if his dentist had not managed to make him a short gold plate with four teeth. Imagine – the course of history changed by toothache or the lack of dentures.

An Open and Shut Case

Perhaps the most famous set of dentures belonged to America's first president, George Washington, who started losing his teeth in his late twenties. By the time of his inauguration in 1789, he possessed no fewer than four sets of dentures, made of gold, ivory, lead, human and animal teeth. The teeth of horses and donkeys were in common use at the time, no doubt impeding the president's speech but giving the phrase 'I heard it from the horse's mouth' a whole new meaning! Washington also had to contend with a spring that helped the dentures open as well as bolts that held them together when his mouth was shut. With this extraordinary contraption lurking in his mouth, it was hardly surprising that the president's default expression was somewhat stern and apparently humourless.

index

picture credits

ART ARCHIVE, NY: 37 top, 92, 95 left

BRIDGEMAN ART LIBRARY: 1, 3, 4, 6–7 (Photo © The Fine Art Society, London, UK), 8–9, 10–11, 15, 16–17, 18 top, 19, 20, 21 top left, 22, 23, 28, 32 top, 33 left, 34 (© National Museum of Wales), 35, 36 top, 37 bottom, 38, 44, 49 (© Devonshire Collection, Chatsworth Reproduced by permission of Chatsworth Settlement Trustees), 50, 53 left, 53 right (Cincinnati Art Museum, Ohio, USA/John J. Emery Endowment), 54 right (Fashion Museum, Bath and North East Somerset Council), 63 right, 64 top, 66 bottom, 68 top, 69 bottom, 72 top, 73, 74–75, 76 left, 77 (Burghley House Collection, Lincolnshire, UK), 80 (© Guildhall Art Gallery, City of London), 81 (Fashion Museum, Bath and North East Somerset Council/Acquired with the assistance of The Art Fund and V&A/Purchase Grant Fund), 84, 85 right, 86 bottom, 87, 88, 90 top, 91 top, 94, 97 bottom (Philadelphia Museum of Art, Pennsylvania, PA, USA/Gift of Mme Elsa Schiaparelli, 1969), 98 top and bottom right, 99, 100, 101 centre right, 112 top, 113, 114, 116, 117 left, 118–19 bottom, 119 top, 126 top right (Germanisches Nationalmuseum, Nuremberg, Germany), 126 bottom (Scottish National Portrait Gallery, Edinburgh, Scotland), 127 top, 127 bottom (© Courtesy of the Warden and Scholars of New College, Oxford), 128 bottom, 129 left, 130–31 (© National Gallery of Scotland, Edinburgh, Scotland), 132 (National Gallery of Victoria, Melbourne, Australia/Everard Studley Miller Bequest), 133 top, 134–35, 134, 136, 137 bottom, 138, 139, 141 right (© Devonshire Collection, Chatsworth Reproduced by permission of Chatsworth Settlement Trustees), 144, 145 left, 154–55, 157, 158 left (Delaware Art Museum, Wilmington, USA/F.V. DuPont Acquisition Fund), 158 right, 159, 160 left (The Israel Museum, Jerusalem, Israel/Bequest of Norbert Schimmel, New York to American Friends of the Israel Museum), 162, 163 top, 164 bottom, 165, 166, 167 right, 168 left, 169 top right, 174, 175 top left, 175 bottom left (© Wallace Collection, London, UK), 176, 177 right, 178, 179, 180, 181 left, 182 left, 186, 187, 188 left, 188 right (Fashion Museum, Bath and North East Somerset Council), 189, 191, 196 left, 202, 203, 204 right (The Israel Museum, Jerusalem, Israel/Vera & Arturo Schwarz Collection of Dada and Surrealist Art), 205, 206, 207 left, 207 right (© British Library Board), 208, 209, 212–13, 212 top, 213, 224, 225 bottom, 228, 235, 236 top, 240, 244 bottom, 247 bottom, front flap cover

CORBIS: 2, 21 bottom, 30, 42, 46, 55, 67 left, 69 top, 71, 79, 102 bottom, 103 bottom, 105 bottom, 122, 147 bottom, 148 top, 163 bottom, 175 right, 184, 190 left and 190–91 centre, 196 right, 198 left, 210, 211 top, 211 bottom, 219 top, 219 bottom, 220 bottom, 221 right, 226–27, 229, 230, 231 right, 232 top, 233, 241 top left and top right, 244 top, 249, back cover, back flap cover

GETTY IMAGES: 27 (bottom), 29, 31, 40, 41 bottom, 43, 45, 47, 51, 52, 57, 58, 59, 67 right, 70, 78, 83, 89 right, 93, 95 right, 96, 101 top right and bottom, 102 top, 103 top left and top right, 104 bottom, 105 top, 106, 108, 112 bottom, 120 top, 121, 123, 125 top, 126 top left, 128 top left and top right, 133 bottom left and bottom right, 137 top, 140, 141 left, 142, 143, 145 right, 146 left, 147 top, 148 bottom, 149, 150, 151, 152, 156 bottom, 160 right, 161, 164 top, 167 left, 168–69, 170, 171, 172–73, 177 left, 182 centre and right, 183, 185, 192, 193, 194 top left and top right and bottom, 195, 199, 204 left, 214 right, 215, 216, 217, 218, 220 top, 221 left, 222–23 centre, 222 left, 223, 225 top, 231 left, 232 bottom, 234, 236 bottom, 237, 241 bottom, 243, 245, 246, 247 top, 248

GRANGER COLLECTION: 39, 41 top, 48, 56, 63 left, 64 bottom, 66 top, 82 right, 85 left, 86 right, 89 left, 109 top, 115, 117 right, 181 right, 197, 198 right, 242

MARTIN HARGREAVES: front cover

SHUTTERSTOCK: endpaper, 18 bottom, 62, 82, 98 bottom left, 104 top, 120 bottom

TOPFOTO: 21 top right, 26–27 top

VICTORIA AND ALBERT MUSEUM, LONDON: 12–13, 24–25, 33 right, 36 bottom, 54 left, 60–61, 65, 68 bottom, 72 bottom, 76 right, 90 bottom, 91 bottom, 97 top, 107, 109 bottom, 124, 125 bottom, 129 right, 146 right, 153, 156, 214, 110–11, 200–201, 238–39

CAPTIONS FOR PRELIMINARY PAGES AND CHAPTER OPENERS

Cover: Bridgeman Art Library. Front flap top and page 3: illustration from a portfolio of watercolours of shoes, German School, twentieth century

Page 1: Fashion design for an evening dress 'Le Pouf' by Paul Poiret (1853–1929)

Pages 2–3: Two models, in a brunette and a blonde wig by Edith Imre, c.1974

Page 4: Portrait of Francois I (1494–1547) by Jean Clouet (1485/90–1540)

Pages 6–7: *Carrying in the Peacock* 1869 by John Dawson Watson (1832–92)

Pages 8–9: Summer fashions for 1836

Pages 10–11: Fashion plate from *Art Gout Beaute*, February 1926

Pages 12–13: Group of models, 1960

Pages 60–61: Peter Robinson silk shoes by Aida Woolf, England, 1914

Pages 74–75: Detail of a gentleman's full dress suit, 1780s–90s

Pages 110–11: White feathered hat, 1960s

Pages 130–31: Portrait of Madame de Pompadour c.1758 by Francois Boucher (1703–70)

Pages 154–55: *An Ancient Custom* by Edwin Longsden Long (1829–91)

Pages 172–73: Wedding lingerie, 1952

Pages 200–201: Model brushing her hair, 1960s

Pages 226–27: Woman with henna tattoos on hands

Pages 238–39: Waspie corset, 1956

APPLE

First published in the UK in 2012 by
Apple Press
7 Greenland Street
London NW1 9EE
United Kingdom

www.apple-press.com

Conceived and produced by
WeldonOwen Publishing
Ground Floor, 10 Northburgh Street,
London, UK EC1V 0AT

weldonowenpublishing.com

Copyright © 2012 Weldon Owen Ltd

Managing Director Sarah Odedina
Editorial Director Russell McLean
Sales Director Laurence Richard
US Sales Director Ellen Towell

Concept and Project Manager Ariana Klepac
Designer Mark Thacker, Big Cat Design
Design Assistants Lucy Katz, Kerry Klinner
Cover Design Jan Bielecki
Picture Researcher Ariana Klepac
Editor Sarah Baker
Text Barbara Cox (Fantastic Footwear, Big Wigs to Beehives, Body Art), Carolyn Sally Jones
(Shape Shifting; Millinery Madness; Bend Me, Shape Me), David and Caroline Stafford
(Introduction, Fantastic Footwear, Ornament & Ostentation, Dandies & Dudes, Greasepaint
& Powder, Under-World), captions by Sarah Baker
Indexer Trevor Matthews
Production Director Dominic Saraceno
Production and Prepress Tristan Hanks

ISBN: 978-1-84543-491-5
Printed and bound in China by 1010 Printing Int Ltd.
The paper used in the manufacture of this book is sourced from wood grown in sustainable forests.
It complies with the Environmental Management System Standard ISO 14001:2004

A WELDON OWEN PRODUCTION

Copyright © 2012 Weldon Owen Ltd